JOHN LA FARGE

Forgive my bad
handwriting. I've
been painting hard
to day, yrs sincerely
Jno. S. Sargent

JOHN LA FARGE

A MEMOIR AND A STUDY

BY

ROYAL CORTISSOZ

BOSTON AND NEW YORK

HOUGHTON MIFFLIN COMPANY

MDCCCCXI

ND 37
L 16 c

TO
THE MEMORY OF
JOHN LA FARGE

PREFACE

My debt to the subject of this memoir must on every page be apparent to the reader, but I wish here to make formal acknowledgment of it. Without La Farge's aid I could not have made my study biographical as well as critical. I have also to thank, for many helpful courtesies, Miss Grace Edith Barnes, in the last ten years of his life his private secretary and appointed by him the executrix of his estate. He made her familiar with much in his career, and the light she has thus been enabled to throw upon it has been generously shared with me.

I am under obligation to Mr. Henry Adams for material of great importance, embracing the letters addressed to him from which I have quoted, the notable analysis extracted from his privately printed "Education of Henry Adams," and some further reflections on his old friend and fellow-traveller in Japan and the South Seas. Mr. James Huneker has been kind enough to lend me a sheaf of La Farge's letters to him. A note from the late Augustus Saint-Gaudens is reproduced by the permission of his son, Homer Saint-Gaudens, and of the Century Company. I have finally to thank the editors of the *Century Magazine* and the *New York Tribune* for authority to make use of passages of my own previously contributed to their respective publications.

ROYAL CORTISSOZ.

New York, February 10, 1911.

TABLE OF CONTENTS

I. A STUDY FOR A PORTRAIT 1

II. ANCESTRY AND EARLY LIFE 41

III. EUROPE 74

IV. THE EVOLUTION OF AN ARTIST 100

V. HALF A CENTURY OF PAINTING 126

VI. GLASS 183

VII. THE OLD MASTER 206

INDEX 265

ILLUSTRATIONS

JOHN LA FARGE IN 1860   *Frontispiece*

From a daguerreotype.

PARADISE VALLEY   24

From the painting in the possession of Gen. Thornton K. Lothrop, Boston.

SLEEPING WOMAN   42

From the early painting destroyed by fire.

WILD ROSES AND WATER LILY   56

From the water-color in the possession of M. B. Philipp, Esq., New York.

THE THREE KINGS   74

From the painting in the possession of the Museum of Fine Arts, Boston.

" NOLI ME TANGERE "   80

From the mural painting in St. Thomas's Church, New York, destroyed by fire. (After an engraving by C. A. Powell.)

CHRIST AND NICODEMUS   90

From the mural painting in Trinity Church, Boston.

JOHN LA FARGE IN 1885   100

From a photograph.

THE ASCENSION   126

From the mural painting in the Church of the Ascension, New York. Reproduced from a photograph in the possession of Miss Serena Rhinelander.

MOSES RECEIVING THE LAW ON MOUNT SINAI   150

From the cartoon for the mural painting in the Supreme Court Room of the Capitol at St. Paul, Minn.

THE PEACOCK WINDOW   184

From the window in the possession of the Art Museum, Worcester, Mass.

FRUIT AND FLOWER GARLAND   194

From the decorative panel painted in wax.

JOHN LA FARGE IN 1902   206

From the portrait by Wilton Lockwood.

WATERFALL IN OUR GARDEN AT NIKKO, JAPAN   220

From the water-color in the possession of H. P. Whitney, Esq., New York.

OFFICIAL PRESENTATION OF GIFTS OF FOOD —
SAMOA   242

From the wash drawing.

Reproduced and somewhat enlarged upon the cover is the seal designed by Rizio Awoki for John La Farge and cut in ivory for him when he was in Japan in 1886. It embodies his surname in Japanese characters.

JOHN LA FARGE

I

A STUDY FOR A PORTRAIT

IT was a characteristic of John La Farge that he had a distaste for the promiscuous shaking of hands. Something in him shrank with almost feminine sensitiveness from all personal contacts, and he was amusingly adroit in evading the particular one to which the ordinary friendly human being is addicted. No visitor was ever allowed to guess that his well-meant salutation had been amiably frustrated. He simply found La Farge with a brush in one hand and a handkerchief in the other, and to dispense with the usual mode of greeting seemed, of course, the most natural thing in the world. Fate made La Farge an artist. By the slightest change of whim she might have made him a diplomat. In that case he would have distinguished himself, above all, by saving his government from everything that looked like coercion. He had a gift for the avoidance of those things that he did not want to do.

The trait testified to neither obstinacy nor a want of sympathy for others. It denoted, rather, a fastidiousness, which, with an idomitable individuality, made him an artist —and a very exacting one — in whatever concerned himself. The ego in him was intense, and, though swathed in the silken folds of an old-world courtesy, it stood implacably upon its rights. This very aloofness of his, these very reserves which counted so heavily in the ordering of his life, have proved, on the other hand, of service to his biographer. La Farge's respect for himself is intertwined, for me, with his respect for his art and for the artistic history which he knew, as a man of his genius could not but know, he had helped to make. I remember visiting an exhibition of his and receiving from him the next day a request that I would go and look at it again. " I have had the distressing red carpet covered with a white gray crash," he said, " all I could find in the hurry, but even that improves the color and tone to such an extent as to make it look differently to me. At least most of the red glare is off." The anxiety which an artist feels for the proper presentation of his work was ever wakeful in La Farge. If he wanted to show you a picture in his studio he would make sure of the hour of the day providing just the right light or he would not show it at all. These precautions, bearing upon the business of the moment, were redoubled in behalf of anything that bore upon the future. Whenever it was a question of establishing on firm ground the record of a specific episode, all those reserves at which I have glanced fell away and he was the willing aid of his interlocutor. I was always writing about his work, and in our purely professional relations he was as helpful as he was punctilious. Upon the freedom of the critic he would have scorned to impose so much as a feather's weight of restraint. In matters of opinion his open-mindedness knew no bounds. But in matters of fact it seemed to him important to get the details straight in even the briefest and most fugitive of chapters. It was to this solicitude for authenticity of statement that I was indebted, through many years, for invaluable communications.

One of these, dating from a time when I was preparing a survey of his career, began with a recollection of something he had read in a book by John Oliver Hobbes, "that very intelligent woman, so American and so 'awfully' Euro-

pean," as he called her. He had forgotten her
exact words, but their meaning, "though better expressed," was more or less as follows:
"That the career of an artist, as we see it,
might be the expression of his professional
intentions or else a record of his personal development, of which the works of art would
merely be the external indication." This
seemed to him worth noting, he said, " even
if it has nothing to do with what you and I are
concerned in." Looking to the personal question actually between us, the question of his
own career, he prefaced a long analysis of his
experience in the painting of landscape with
these words : —

"I have, of course, no idea of how you are
going to handle the facts of my life as an artist,
externally or internally. What I am anxious
about is to tell you what I know, and what I
think, of certain things I have done. Whether
they are known or appear to others as they do
to me is another matter. The mere facts, however, are matters of date or of record, and are
not things of appreciation except in the sense
of gauging their importance. In the different
cases of a good deal of my work these points
of how and why I came to do a thing are im-

portant to me because they are usually unre-
lated to anything being done outside at that
time."

The drift of this passage explains why it is
worth while, and, in fact, helpful to a clearer
understanding of La Farge's character, for me
to describe in some detail the origin of this
volume. He wished to write his reminiscences
and made fitful attempts to do so, but ill-health
handicapped him, and constantly, when he had
the energy and was in the mood, his work as
an artist enforced the first claim. Several years
ago it occurred to me to bring together much
of the criticism which I had devoted to his
work, and he received the idea with cordial
sympathy. I told him that for such a mono-
graph certain biographical details were essential, and he cheerfully agreed to put them in
my hands. As time went on he developed an
intense interest in the book, coming to regard
it as a kind of repository for the recollections
and reflections which, in other circumstances,
he might have embodied in a book of his own.
We had been close friends for some twenty
years and there was a perfect trust between
us. He gave me freely what he had already
put into manuscript, and continued to write, as

he had written in other times, memories of his life and his practice as an artist for me to use.

When something recurred to him that he thought belonged to the narrative he would send it to me in a letter, or I would receive a message like this: "Perhaps to-morrow, at some off hour, you might be tempted to come and be surprised, and perhaps entertained, by a little story I have to tell. It's queer, and worth turning out of one's way for. I thought of Sunday, because it is labelled a day of rest. I forgot that such people as you or I may choose that day otherwise." In another note he remarks, apropos of our meeting soon thereafter, that he perhaps will have to tell me "some more curiosities," and in still another he says, "I had an absurdity on my mind which will keep many days." As his interest grew, and the book took on more and more of the character of a record, he showed me more and more of the helpfulness and even anxiety of a collaborator. Once, when I had been too absorbed in other duties to go on with the task, he wrote saying, "I have no news ever from you. Evidently you are not writing up my life." Nevertheless we found many occasions

to sit down together for conversations, lasting
far into the night, of which it was understood
between us that I would afterwards take such
notes as memory made possible. Those were
happy evenings, continued assiduously until
by and by illness brought them to an end.
Presently, too, from the same cause, our meet-
ings by daylight were given more to casual
talk than to the reconstruction of old times and
scenes. But that historical sense of his to which
I referred at the outset never left him, and
down to the end his letters carried on the
thread of our subject, or spoke of further passages that he had planned. In one of them,
dating from his last illness, he says, "I intend
writing you a long, long screed to continue the
autobiography of which you are to make a
'Biograph.' . . . I still hope to see you some
day," and only a few weeks before his death
he wrote me again, thus: "I must answer
your letter in full, there is so much to take up,
both for us here and for the record abroad.
But it is only to-day that I see a chance to get
a stenographer for dictation and then you will
be deluged."

The deluge never came. There was rest,
instead, for that kindling brain and that inde-

fatigable hand. From the citations I have made
the reader will understand my desire to use
in the following pages, wherever possible,
La Farge's words, rather than my own, and
he will realize, too, the peculiar sense of responsibility with which I have undertaken to
carry out my task. This book is, in some sort,
the fulfilment of a purpose shared by La Farge
and myself. The reader who suspects that it
has been written in affection will not be far
wrong. From the exaggerations of uncritical
hero-worship biographers sometimes go to the
other extreme, and, out of a solemnly expressed respect for "the verdict of posterity,"
hesitate to give free play to the faith that is
in them. Doubtless this is judicious, but doubtless, too, it smacks a little of evasion. I am
abundantly aware that I have no business with
the verdict of posterity, but of one thing I am
convinced, and that is that La Farge was a
great artist, and, into the bargain, a man to
love. It was my good fortune to know him
intimately for a long period and to be with
him often, alone, in talk which knew no bar-
riers. Our friendship was never even momentarily disturbed by so much as the shadow of
a shadow. It is with grateful loyalty to a be-

loved master in the things of the mind that I
have sought to draw his portrait.

It is at this stage of my undertaking that
I wish I could achieve the impossible, and, as
a preliminary toward the recital of many of
La Farge's own sayings, so paint him that the
reader might see and hear him. The charm of
La Farge was prodigiously heightened by the
originality and distinction of his countenance,
the vividness of the appeal made through his
carriage, his typical gestures, and a quiet but
curiously rich and characterful voice. He had
the thinker's skull, amply domed, and his dark
brown hair, extraordinarily fine and silky, retained its color long after age had set its mark
upon him. In fact, it was only very late, when
he had entered upon the final struggle with
illness, that the graying of his hair became
noticeable. His features both harmonized with
the pure structure of his head and gave it elements of strangeness, like the accents placed
here and there by genius in a great sculptured
portrait. The nose was long, straight, and powerful, with nostrils well curved, delicate in
texture, very firmly defined, the nose of a
man of breeding. It descended from between
strongly marked brows, which, with the fine

green-gray eyes, gave the face its most arrest-
ing note of individuality, though the ears, too,
large and beautifully set, were full of character. His eyes were generously lidded and
seemed to come forward from their big, deep
sockets with a rounded weightiness again suggesting a statue. They were opened wide in
moments of astonishment, of indignation and
irony, but I chiefly remember them peering
through half-closed lids and expressive of reflection, of brooding enquiry. The straightly
drawn mouth, with lips that were firm but
could be very mobile, and the solid chin spoke
of determination, authority, and an unshakable
self-confidence. His skin was close-grained
and smooth, with a soft warmth of tint difficult
to describe, for it partook of the olive hue of
the Southern Latin races and of that quality,
suggestive of wax or of parchment, which you
will often find in the scholar of any clime. His
was one of those complexions which seem, in
fact, to take their subdued richness of color
from an inner, spiritual glow.

He was a man of good height, though lat-
terly a stooping habit withdrew attention from
the fact that he was full six feet tall, as it like-
wise disguised his possession of an unusually

deep chest. His feet were small and well
formed, long and slender, like his hands, and
those, with their aristocratic fingers, were the
hands of an artist in the fullest sense of the
traditional phrase. His figure left an impression of leanness, until you came to observe its
good proportions and to realize that he was not
what is usually called a bony type, but simply
a man whose laborious and refined habit of
life had naturally kept him in spare condition.
Refinement in its very essence was subtly proclaimed in all the details of his appearance and
in all his little idiosyncrasies. I saw him, occasionally, in other colors, in gray or in brown,
but as a rule he is associated in my mind with
black. Whatever he wore testified to an intense fastidiousness. Linen and silk could not
be of too fine a texture for him. He lived
softly, as the saying goes, not from an indo-
lent or sensuous taste, but because the artist
in him rebelled against the second best or the
thing rough to the touch. He would be as exacting about his handkerchiefs, say, as about
the implements on his painting table, or the
Japanese paper on which he made so many
of his drawings. His garments were like his
demeanor, unthought of by him, in a sense,

but part of his belief that life should be gracious and dignified, neat, well ordered, and always protected, somehow, from carelessness and disrespect. And never for an instant did his conformity to a severe standard of taste chill or otherwise overpower his sheer delightfulness.

The photograph of him which serves as a frontispiece to this volume shows how handsome, handsome indeed to the point of fascination, he was in his youth. My friend, the late Katharine Prescott Wormeley, the translator of Balzac, knew him well in old Newport days, and, telling me how interesting he then was, she laid stress upon the fact that he was notably picturesque. He was always that, but in his prime, when I first knew him, with the picturesqueness softened and given as it were a rich reposeful tone, by something subtly prelatical. The first time I ever dined with him, long ago, we sat alone at one of the vast tables in the old Brevoort House, taken care of by a waiter whose sedateness and efficiency marked him as an embodiment of the tradition of that once famous hotel. La Farge fitted beautifully into that old " Washington Square " picture, a type of our older regime, the calm, authorita-

tive and exquisitely urbane man of the world.
But even then I saw his ceremonious habit
tempered and lightened by the *franchise* of the
artist; and, only a few evenings later, I had a
deeper initiation into his charm when, in the
big shadowy studio he had for half a century
in the old Tenth Street building, we discussed
by candle light a meal improvised on one of
the working tables by his Japanese retainer.
Then I saw better how La Farge was, what I
always found him thereafter down to the day
of his death, a blend of entirely mundane so-
phistication with the easy, informal, lovable
traits of a man so whole-heartedly given to
artistic and intellectual things that, while he
valued forms and conventions and could not
do without them, he could not for the life of
him overestimate their importance. When he
had shown you the necessary courtesies he
settled down to talk, and in place of the tone
of the drawing-room he gave you that which
belongs to the romantic world of art.

I have heard some brilliant talkers, Whistler amongst them, but I have never heard one
even remotely comparable to La Farge. He
knew nothing of the glittering, phrase-making
habit of the merely clever man, to whom the

condensation of a bit of repartee into an epi-
gram is a triumph. "I am not a clever man,"
he once said to me, "but sometimes I do clever
things. I think when that happens it is the
work of the dæmon of Socrates." He gave
me a droll instance. He was dictating to a
typewriter who made a mess of the names of
some Chinese gods. "Like a flash I said to her,
'Miss X., you have put in here the name of
your best man.' She blushed violently and ad-
mitted it." He paused. "They often do that,"
he added, with one of his understanding smiles.
There were often, by the way, such flashes of
innocent fun as this in his conversation, but
he held you, of course, on a far higher plane.
There he practised a serene eloquence, ranging
over fields so spacious that in addition to the
weighty substance of his talk he stimulated
the listener as with a sense of large issues, of
brave venturings into seas of thought. He had
seen the world, he had known a multitude of
men and things, and this rich experience re-
acted upon his nature. But his complexity was
a central possession, it was of the very texture
of his soul. There went with it, too, a peculiar poise, a strange, self-centred calm. His
pronounced sympathy for the East was easily

understood. He liked its attitude of contemplation. His own habit was meditative. But where his individuality made a still further claim was in the direction of a tremendous intellectual and spiritual activity.

To sit with him in fervid talk on a thousand things was to feel, presently, that he flung out a myriad invisible tentacles of understanding, electric filaments which in an instant identified him with the subject of his thought and made him free of its innermost secrets. And what he gathered through these magical processes he brought back and put before you, slowly, with an almost oracular deliberation, but in such living words and with such an artistic balancing of his periods that you saw what he saw, felt what he felt, and waited in positively tense enjoyment for the unfolding of the next mental picture. I have spoken of his periods. The phrase is, perhaps, not quite exact, for a sentence of La Farge's might carry you almost anywhere before arriving at its goal. The goal was always reached. The certainty of that consummation was one more of his spells. You watched and waited in absolute security but sometimes a little breathlessly, for La Farge was a past master of the parenthesis and he

hated to let go of his collateral lines of thought.
It was as though he glanced wistfully at them,
as at ripples in the wake of his leading motive,
and grudged their loss. There were moments
when he would pause to recapture them.
There were others when, with a smile, he let
them fade, as one who would say, whimsically,
" We could have got some profitable variations out of that theme."

What he said was inspiring, but there was
an added stimulus for the listener in this con-
versational mode of his ; by itself it fostered
liberal thought and especially gave you the
warm and thrilling sensation of being in the
presence of pure genius. It is the singularity
of that genius that I am particularly anxious
to enforce and hence I am glad to be permitted to quote the finest analysis of it that I
know. This was written by Mr. Henry Adams, the historian, with whom La Farge made
his Japanese and South Sea journeys. It occurs
in " The Education of Henry Adams," the
work which the author wrote in the third person. Thus it runs : —

" Of all the men who had deeply affected
their friends since 1850 John La Farge was
certainly the foremost, and for Henry Adams,

who had sat at his feet since 1872, the question how much he owed to La Farge could be answered only by admitting that he had no standard to measure it by. Of all his friends La Farge alone owned a mind complex enough to contrast against the commonplaces of American uniformity, and in the process had vastly perplexed most Americans who came in contact with it. The American mind, — the Bostonian as well as the Southern or Western, — likes to walk straight up to its object, and assert or deny something that it takes for a fact; it has a conventional approach, a conventional analysis, and a conventional conclusion, as well as a conventional expression, all the time loudly asserting its unconventionality. The most disconcerting trait of John La Farge was his reversal of the process. His approach was quiet and indirect; he moved round an object, and never separated it from its surroundings; he prided himself on faithfulness to tradition and convention; he was never abrupt and abhorred dispute. His manners and attitude towards the universe were the same, whether tossing in the middle of the Pacific Ocean sketching the trade-wind from a whale-boat in the blast of sea-sickness,

or drinking the *cha-no-yu* in the formal rites
of Japan, or sipping his cocoa-nut cup of Kava
in the ceremonial of Samoan chiefs, or reflect-
ing under the sacred bo-tree at Anaradjpura.

"One was never quite sure of his whole
meaning until too late to respond, for he had
no difficulty in carrying different shades of
contradiction in his mind. As he said of his
friend Okakura, his thought ran as a stream
runs through grass, hidden perhaps but always there; and one felt often uncertain in
what direction it flowed, for even a contradiction was to him only a shade of difference, a
complementary color, about which no intelligent artist would dispute. Constantly he re-
pulsed argument:— 'Adams, you reason too
much!' was one of his standing reproaches
even in the mild discussion of rice and man-
goes in the warm night of Tahiti dinners. He
should have blamed Adams for being born in
Boston. The mind resorts to reason for want
of training, and Adams had never met a perfectly trained mind.

"To La Farge, eccentricity meant convention; a mind really eccentric never betrayed
it. True eccentricity was a tone, — a shade,
— a *nuance*, — and the finer the tone, the

truer the eccentricity. Of course all artists hold more or less the same point of view in their art, but few carry it into daily life, and often the contrast is excessive between their art and their talk. One evening Humphreys Johnston, who was devoted to La Farge, asked him to meet Whistler at dinner. La Farge was ill, — more ill than usual even for him, — but he admired and liked Whistler and insisted on going. By chance, Adams was so placed as to overhear the conversation of both, and had no choice but to hear that of Whistler, which engrossed the table. At that moment the Boer war was raging, and, as every one knows, on that subject Whistler raged worse than the Boers. For two hours he declaimed against England, — witty, declamatory, extravagant, bitter, amusing and noisy; but in substance what he said was not merely commonplace, — it was true! That is to say, his hearers, including Adams and, as far as he knew, La Farge, agreed with it all, and mostly as a matter of course; yet La Farge was silent, and this difference of expression was a difference of art. Whistler in his art carried the sense of *nuance* and tone far beyond any point reached by La Farge, or

even attempted; but in talk he showed, above
or below his color-instinct, a willingness to
seem eccentric where no real eccentricity, unless perhaps of temper, existed.

" This vehemence, which Whistler never
betrayed in his painting, La Farge seemed to
lavish on his glass. . . . In conversation La
Farge's mind was opaline with infinite shades
and refractions of light, and with color toned
down to the finest gradations. In glass it was
insubordinate; it was renaissance; it asserted
his personal force with depth and vehemence
of tone never before seen. He seemed bent
on crushing rivalry."

The "infinite shades and refractions of
light" which Mr. Adams describes had the
effect of etching upon the hearer's mind pictures of a phenomenal completeness and vividness. La Farge had the power of the necro-
mancer to take you, as though on a carpet out
of the "Arabian Nights," away from the world
of prose into one of thought and beauty. An
instance salient amongst my recollections is
connected with the opening of the Saint-Gaudens memorial exhibition, at the Metropolitan
Museum in New York, one night in March,
1908. He and the sculptor had been life-long

friends and he had an affectionate desire to
pay him the tribute of sharing in this formal
observance, but he was not well and shrank
from going alone. We went together. On the
way there in a cab he told me, apropos of his
walking stick, which had been cut for him by
a cannibal chief, some of his memories of the
Fiji Islands. He was struck by the queer mixture there of civilized and barbaric traits.
Speaking of the good breeding of the natives
he described the resemblance of some of them
to the well-set-up, hard clubman of New York
or London, who looks after himself with un-
abashed selfishness but in a gentlemanly way.
He told me how he and his companion upon
those South Sea travels rejoiced over the report of the British Governor, who, on a certain occasion, was accepting the submission
of the chiefs. This functionary was not alto-
gether sure about giving his countenance to
one member of the company, for, he said,
"He is not a gentleman." "It was so perfectly true," said La Farge, and went on in an
analysis of the barbaric character so entranc-
ing that our arrival at the Museum induced a
kind of shock.

He was enormously interested and pleased

with what he found there — and very amusing on the beauty of "the living sculpture"
which filled the great hall — but after he had
held court for a little while, talking with the
people he knew, we came away. What im-
pressed me about the whole episode was its
note of dedication to a cherished friend. Ill
and tired as he was, he had by his presence
given testimony to the faithfulness with which
he held the memory of Saint-Gaudens in his
heart. It was late by the time we had found
our cab; but for talk it was as though the
night had only just begun, and all the way
home I listened to probably the most remarkable piece of easy, natural, but truly inspiring eloquence the gods could ever give me.
It was discursive, as usual, infinitely parenthetical, but it possessed that unity which, as
I have said, he always secured. He told me
about a journey made by his friend Okakura
in the East, a visit to an historic Chinese monastery far from cities. The traveller was wel-
comed in a bare little room by a priest who
sat down upon the floor to a stringed instrument and spoke, as it were, through its music.
Then followed different ceremonies, which
were somehow made as real to me as obser-

vances in a Western church; after that came
the count of Okakura's full days, the priestly
farewell, spoken again in music, and, at last,
the sacramental bowl lifted to the lips of the
speeding guest under an ancient tree some
distance from the monastery. In the night
outside our cab the noises of the street seemed
to sink into silence, the ranks of commonplace
buildings to give way to a far landscape, and,
literally, I seemed to hear the thin notes rising from beneath the mysterious priest's yellow fingers. Again, at La Farge's door, one
seemed to be wakened from a dream.

I should be leaving my tale but half told
if I failed to lay stress upon the fact that the
compelling glamour of La Farge's talk, of
these reveries made articulate, was deepened
by the character of his physiognomy, which,
true to the varied impulses of his being, had
the power to stir one, in different times and
moods, to very different mental associations.
In a characteristic attitude of earlier years he
stays in my memory as a singularly alert
and nervous figure, with hands thrust in his
pockets, head jerked back, mouth twisted,
and the muscles of his face taut as he stood
round-eyed with comic amazement — good-

humoredly astounded at the eternal banality
of things. He seemed very modern then and
very human. Later, when he had begun to pay
his debt to time, the wonderfully modelled
head, with its great brow, sank a little between
the shoulders, and, as he burrowed down into
a big chair and gloomed gently at his companion through the rims of his wide spectacles, he
looked like some majestic dignitary musing
in the obscure recesses of an Oriental temple.
The subdued ivory tint which distinguished
his complexion in his old age especially contributed to this impression, and then, too, his
profound passion for the East made it in some
inexplicable fashion the easier thus to visual-
ize him. Again there were times when you felt
that he wore the mask of an old Italian priest.
In the Renaissance he would have been a Cardinal statesman, one of those militant princes
of the Church who triumphed, however, by
astuteness rather than by force of arms, and
Mantegna would have rejoiced to paint his
portrait, as Pisanello would with gladness
have made his rare profile immortal within the
narrow limits of a medal. The impenetrability
stamped upon his face would only have made
the appeal to their imagination the stronger.

Paradise Valley

A habit of secretiveness, when it is not ren-
dered ignoble by relation to petty things, will
put a *patina* of mystery upon the personality
of a man. La Farge, who wore this impalpable
armor, was made still more baffling by something alien and exotic in his nature. His appearance denoted subtle alliances with things
outside our everyday life. Beside him entirely
admirable people, who never in their lives
committed a solecism and had brains into the
bargain, still seemed a little crude and flat. I
used often to reflect as we sat talking together
that his being in New York at all was an incongruity, a sacrifice, and a frustration. He
should have dwelt in Paris and spent Olym-
pian evenings there, discussing monumental
decorations with Puvis, or Italian mysticism
with Gebhart, or Latin literature with Boissier, or religious origins with Renan and Salomon Reinach. Best of all, he should have held
endless discourse on everything under the
sun with that "pawky Benedictine" — as he
himself might have been called — Anatole
France. He should have been another Pierre
Loti, cosseted by the State and sent up and
down the world in a warship to collect sensations. On his return, as he donned the palm

leaves of an Academician and accepted the greetings of respectfully attentive colleagues, he would have interpreted to them the genius of remote peoples with an insight and a philosophic wisdom of which Loti never dreamed.

If I speak of him as a spiritual exile it is not because he lacked, here, the company of his peers. A man who could hope for even one encounter in a year or two with a friend such as Clarence King, for example, might reconcile himself to a desert island. But La Farge needed a frame, a tradition, an environment part and parcel of the sequence of civilization to which he belonged. With his work to do he would have been happy anywhere, and he was indubitably happy and content as an American. Yet the spirit of old Europe or that of the older Orient was forever pulling at his heartstrings, and, though he never had a syllable of complaint to make about his destiny, I was often conscious of an unspoken ruefulness in him, a half-amused wonder as to whether, somewhere else in the world, there might not be springs at which it would be a little more satisfying to drink. He loved his country. If shortsightedness had not disqualified him he would have gone to the front in the Civil War.

His fellow artists know with what generosity
and effectiveness he gave himself to the advancement of our school. Nevertheless my
sense of his detachment from his surroundings
will not down. For all his interest in them,
his understanding of them, and, at many
points, his sympathy for them, his inner life
was lived in a singular isolation.

This never betrayed his sense of proportion.
He saw life and himself too justly for that and
he was too ready to smile at the fatuity of any
man's imagining that he was too big for his
opportunity. In his smile, kindly and quizzi-
cal, there was, before all else, complete comprehension. His humor was not precisely
saturnine, but it was very subtile and a little
malin, too intellectualized for it to seem the
mere gayety of the ordinary man in high spirits. He practised the delicate art of thinking
as constantly and as naturally as he breathed,
and this gave a conscious direction to even the
most spontaneous flashes of his fun. All the
relations of life were dramatized in that quick
brain of his, so swiftly, and with so far-reach-
ing a *flair* for their last, most evanescent re-
verberations or implications, that out of the
smallest episode he could wring shades of sen-

sation undreamed of by another observer —
or by the victim himself. Every word uttered,
every letter written, every move made in the
recondite game of life, though not long medi-
tated, had, at all events, its sufficiently pon-
dered purpose. He never discharged an arrow
in the dark. It sometimes, too, reached its
mark when his aim seemed most casual.

As I write these lines I realize that they
need, not correction, but extension into that
atmosphere of mere human friendliness which
robs gravity of its forbidding aspect and turns
an eminent man into an endearing companion.
La Farge could be, in his way, jolly. He liked
now and then to have young people about him
and to laugh with them. He adored "limer-
icks," when they were killingly preposterous;
and if he knew how to smile with consummate
meaning he knew also how to chuckle, a gift
with which cynicism is hardly compatible. Our
evenings together might be never so absorbing in the seriousness of their topics, but there
was always room in them for mirth. There
was an old joke between us that cigars to be
good must be large, fat, and of a fairly rich
flavor. I would receive an invitation from him,
couched in his never-failing terms of eigh-

teenth-century courtesy, as in one summons to a new apartment he had taken — "the room is clean, that's one thing, not much else in its favor except your coming " — and then there would be the familiar allusion to the tobacco without which a symposium was supposed to be unthinkable. "I have cigars," he would write, "decent whiskey, some poor champagne, and average brandy — enough to put aside a few moments." We soon put them aside. With meticulous care he would see that all was in order, especially the matches, and then, in clouds of smoke, we would forget the liquids. Apropos of the latter, by the way, he told me that only once in his life had his taste in wine exceeded his discretion. With the late Russell Sturgis, himself a seasoned connoisseur, he sat down to enjoy some notable Burgundies. The feast had been appointed for that purpose. They gave their minds and palates to so many vintages as to so many works of art. Their heads were untouched. Ideas came only the more speedily. Conversation had never been more luminous or delightful. But when, with immense satisfaction in their evening, the diners sought to rise, their legs calmly refused to perform their accustomed office.

That was all that had happened, and that, though temporarily embarrassing, was inordinately funny. The mere memory of the incident was a source of huge amusement to La Farge.

There was one trait of his into which all the rest were gathered up, his love of his work; and what a tremendous driving force it was may be seen the more clearly if we consider the heavy handicap of ill health that he carried. In his letters there are constant allusions to this subject. As far back as 1896 I find him saying, "It is a very broken down person who writes to you," and on another occasion he writes, "I feel as if I had a personal devil after me for the last eighteen months." For years it was a common experience with him to do much of his writing in bed. In fact, a certain physical disability dogged his footsteps practically all his life long. In the fall of 1908, when news of his having been ill got into print, he sent me a long letter for publication in the *Tribune*, and in it gave this account of the burden against which he had had to contend: —

"As I am led into talking about myself, I wish to note a matter which is interesting to me, and which is also interesting in a general

manner, and this is that I have been off and on
an ill man since the years 1866 and 1867. I
was paralyzed by what later was supposed to
be lead poisoning, which affects some of us
painters very much, and which can be continued in the practice of the art of what is
called 'stained glass,' where lead is much used
and fills the air, and the hands, etc., of the
people engaged. Notwithstanding, I have
done, I think, as much as any artist since this
illness. Indeed, to point a moral, I think that
such a condition is an enormous incentive for
struggle. The lame foot of the late Lord Byron
was part of his equipment for becoming a great
English poet. The same for many of the painters — take Mr. Whistler, for instance, and
one of the greatest, Delacroix, always an ill
man, from a similar trouble to mine. The result has been the same for me from my lame-
ness, which has not always been apparent, but
which is always there, and which city life and
the necessary use of a cab (at which my friends
laugh) do not tend to diminish. In the open
air of far-away countries one is better of everything, and I have walked and been in the
saddle for days.

"Some thirty odd years ago, when I undertook the beginning of decorative work in churches by painting Trinity Church, my kindly assistants had always to help me up the 30-foot ladder on to the great scaffoldings. Not to mention Saint-Gaudens, who is dead, and others, Mr. Maynard, for instance, will remember our conditions. This did not prevent my painting on the wall, slung on a narrow board sixty feet above the floor of the church, with one arm passed around a rope and holding my palette, while the other was passed around the other rope, and I painted on my last figure, eighteen feet high, which had to be finished the next morning at 7 o'clock. I painted five hours that night in that way, and painted for twenty-one hours out of the twenty-four. For a sick man, you can see that the strain was well met, and many times since I have had to go through this physical strain of painting a big picture on the wall from the scaffoldings."

Nothing could shake his courageous tenacity. Even when he was laid on his back he would continue to labor. With neuritis in his right hand, so that "even opening a newspaper has been hard," he wrote me saying, "and yet I have done things. I hope the bad luck has not been reflected in the work." When he could not work in bed he read there. "The proof that I have not given up things," he wrote me, "is that I am trying to find a copy of Huysmans' 'Trois Primitifs.' Every one knows it. No one has it. I have scoured town as far as I can. . . . If I am not too faint I'd like to see you." By good luck I had the book, and, faint as he was, he battened on it. But no reading could beguile him into compromising with bodily weakness and staying in bed an instant longer than he could help. Irresistibly his work would get him on his feet, and, if there is something painful, there is also something gallant and exhilarating, about the way in which he was forever pulling himself together, to go on with the labors which made, first and last, his truest happiness.

Mingled with his ruling passion there was a sense of duty. Others were involved in his undertakings. There was the point of honor to remember, the obligation to be fulfilled. Thus he writes me: "The whirligig of time has brought its annoyances. Suddenly I am more or less on my back. . . . I have a multitudinousness of ills and pains that must be cared for *seriously*; because besides the things themselves I have a lot of work to carry out, and I am reminded that I am part of a machine like any other cog." At another time, complaining of "a series of strange failures of health," he nevertheless goes on to rejoice that he is back at his easel, exclaiming, "to-day I am very proud, because I have been able to stand up and paint. It seems a sort of dream when I look back upon the last few weeks; the painting seems to be the unreal thing." Telling me in one of his letters how much he has had to put aside, he explains that "this is because I have decided to go on with my work and I have to treat myself as a broken-down automobile which has still to get back home. . . . I vary intervals of work by giving up everything and vice versa." But sometimes nature rebelled and he had to ease the strain, whether he would or no. Here is an illustration of his reluctance to slacken work, though he knew that he had to do so : —

"I am writing to you in bed, for I shall be driven when I get up. . . . All the spare strength and all the time of to-day will be given to so finishing my two big panels that I may get them to the Century Club to-mor-row. . . . Should it take your fancy, come in and see me at the studio before that, even though I am at work to-day. . . . If you prefer seeing my two big traps, etc., in studio light and a little unfinished, all right. This, of course, is irregular and if Miss Barnes, my watchdog, were here, I should be informed that I was wasting painting time. But I know that I can't pull at it all day — I am not strong enough. . . . 'There you are,' as Harry James has it."

The admission that he must nurse his resources is only wrung from him by *force majeure*. His ardor for work was so intense that he rebelled in something like wrathful bewilderment when pain and illness gripped him. "Why?" he asked me once, with sorrowful indignation, "Why am I ill and why old?" No other mischance of fortune could seem to him half so cruel or so unnecessary. But, after all, it did not conclusively matter. Down to the end he was full of projects and splendid resolutions, intent upon carrying on his service to beauty the moment that strength returned. He knew that with energy restored the mere piling up of the years meant nothing. In the letter from which I have already given the story of his early and ever-recurring illness he goes on

to register in this way his belief in the pro-
ductivity of old age : —

"The operations of art are largely intellectual, and can be met by a life devoted
to study and the acquirement of the proper
knowledge. We have had and have still a
good many distinguished artists who go on
with their work late. The Frenchmen of the
fifties and sixties persisted far up into the seventies and eighties, and that is without our
daring to think of the past far away, when
Michael Angelo and Titian worked up to a very
late period of life. Most of the great paintings
of Titian, as you know, such as the marvellous
'Charles V,' and I do not know how many
hundreds of others, were painted after his sev-
enty-fifth year. In fact, as we know, he passed
away at ninety-nine, owing to the pestilence
which attacked Venice. As an artist friend of
mine used to say, if it had not been for that
he might still be painting. I cannot hope for
such a lengthy chance of doing work and en-
joying that wonderful art of expressing one's
emotion, but I think that I may still go on for
some little while."

He was sustained in his hard-fought cam-
paign by his sense of humor and his unfail-

ing appreciation of the little things of life, the pleasant little things. As in the experience of that acquaintance of Dr. Johnson, Oliver Edwards, "Cheerfulness was always breaking in." The moment that suffering began to pass away he was ready for anything. Writing to me at such a point of improvement, he gayly says, "I am coming to that stage of being better at which my Samoan friends like a little raw fish. You know they have a special word in their language for that desire." When our smoking bouts had, perforce, been interrupted, and he had to say "I am still off my smoke," he would talk with much joking about the prospects of his soon getting back to his cigar. In sickness, too, nothing cheered him more than a word of goodwill and appreciation. He liked to know when his work was valued. Once when Miss Barnes had gone abroad upon a holiday and was in London, Alma-Tadema told her how the Kaiser had been at his house a day or two before. The imperial visitor had admired everything he saw in that famous studio and dwelling, but, as he left, he told the artist that the one thing he envied him and would like to carry away was the window by La Farge that he possessed. La Farge was

greatly tickled over this, and at the same time
he wrote to me with glee about a proposal
then afoot — Dr. Bode wanted to make an
exhibition of his glass at the Berlin Museum.
The plan ultimately fell through, but that it
was thought of pleased La Farge. A creative
artist of his calibre does not need to be told
when he has done well, but he was too big
a man to assume a foolish superiority to the
generous recognition of his contemporaries.
He told me how Rossetti, seeing something
of his at the house of a friend, wrote to him
over here a handsome message of encourage-
ment. It was the first thing of the sort in his
life, he said, and it was really helpful to him.
A passage in one of his late letters shows how
this feeling of thankfulness for friendly stimulus lasted with him through life. "I wish to
tell you," he wrote, "that I have a great com-
plimentary message from Rodin and feel much
set up."

He had the fundamental modesty of the
man of genius, a deep consciousness of how
far short of his aim every painter, no matter
how great, has always fallen. A note as of
noble despair, of fine humility before the magnitude of the painter's task, creeps into one

of his last letters. Writing out of doors he says:—

"I feel in every part of each second that Nature is almost too beautiful — all of it, every millionth part of it, light and color and shapes. . . . Each little or big blade of grass in front of me, and there are millions, has its shape and its composition. The colors are exquisite. . . . As I lift my eyes from the wonderful green (never painted yet by man) I see a pale blue sky with pale cumulus clouds, white, with violet shadows, and on the other side the blue is deep, and, in an hour, shall be deeper yet."

Before visions like that, and his life was full of them, he was truly humble, reverent before the miracles of nature, and imbued, too, with a sense of the sacredness of his calling. He knew what desperate difficulties lie between the painter and the adequate expression of even a tithe of what he sees in the endless pageant of earth. But he knew, too, what his gifts were, the singleness of his purpose, and, above all, the rapture of achievement. These and other emotions, analysis of which belongs more properly to a later phase of my study, confirmed in him that respect for himself to which I referred at the outset. If a triumph in his art gave him joy it also made him proud.

Every reader of Landor's life will remember the wretched litigation which drove him from Bath in his old age and sent him back to Florence, where the English minister, Lord Normanby, with others, took note of the scandal and acted accordingly. To the leader of his enemies the fiery poet sent a memorable rebuke, the sting of which resided in its close: " I am not inobservant of distinctions. You by the favour of a Minister are Marquis of Normanby. I by the grace of God am Walter Savage Landor."

La Farge was like that.

II

ANCESTRY AND EARLY
LIFE

WHEN La Farge was a young man, travelling in Europe, he met at Copenhagen a member of a Danish family of French origin, M. Jean de Joncquière. The ancestors of this gentleman had left France in the time of Henri Quatre. The family jealously preserved the letters written by that monarch to an old soldier of their house, who had fought under him, and La Farge's friend, though he had never seen the land of his forefathers, possessed its language and cherished its memories. Aware of the visitor's French blood he said to him, " Never forget your descent. It is a privilege to have an ideal nationality." La Farge remembered. He had, indeed, a lively sense of the privilege of carrying French blood in his veins. It colored his whole temperament and undoubtedly determined, in a measure, the movement of his mind. I was with him once, not long after he had been talking with a kinswoman of his, who was fond of hunting after odd things, who had wondered why the name of Abraham was in the family, and had asked him if it suggested any Jewish ancestors. La Farge was not sure but that it did and he mused quizzically on the subject; but it interested him only as something very remote and vague. That he came of a line of Frenchmen was all he really knew or cared to know.

He cared, I think, not only in obedience to the instinct of race but because his ancestral history touched his imagination. La Farge lived by imagination and this fact is my governing principle in traversing his life. The place of his birth, the houses he lived in, the sources of his education, the journeys he made — such things as these count in his biography only as they bear upon the development of his character and the fertilizing of his brilliant intellect. The memories that he rescued from the past embraced, of course, the simple everyday incidents that are common to most children and young men; but as he looked back at his boyhood he could see how the special influences at work therein had given a special turn to his way of thinking and feeling. Especially he recognized the formative effect at

Sleeping Woman

that time of associations which, if then but half understood, nevertheless enlarged his perspective and gave him an obscure consciousness of contact with exceptional conditions. Through his father he touched hands with participants in the great military collisions and political upheavals of the late eighteenth and early nineteenth centuries. There was romance in the possession of a father who had felt the shock of the French Revolution and had been in peril of his life in scenes of tropical adventure.

It was in 1806 that Jean-Frédéric de la Farge had come to this country, a lucky refugee from the massacre in San Domingo. He had come to the island as an Ensign in the naval expedition which landed General Leclerc to effect the seizure and transportation of Toussaint. Young La Farge was wounded in the action through which his ship pierced the British blockade, but evidently this only heightened his spirits, for he presently exchanged his ensignship for a lieutenancy in the army and was thenceforth in the thick of the turmoil. He was captured by Guerrier on one of his expeditions, falling into a trap, " very much as it might be in the Philippines to-day," and did not regain his freedom until, on the eve of the massacre, he and two other whites succeeded in evading the negroes, and, starting in a small boat, ultimately boarded a ship bound for Philadelphia. It does not appear that he had any thought of returning to France and a life of action. Arrived in America he subsided into civil life, married, and prospered. His wife was the daughter of M. Binsse de Saint-Victor, who had himself at one time been a planter in San Domingo, a Frenchman of the old régime, whose family name will recur more than once in this narrative. The elder John La Farge, as I gather he called himself in his adopted country, had laid down his arms but had lost nothing of his energy. While the dramatic passages in his career remained but a memory, flinging their atmosphere of hazard and of historic events over his family life, he gave himself up to business and the making of a fortune. He came to own a plantation in Louisiana and extensive properties in Jefferson and Lewis counties in New York. A village not many miles from Watertown still bears his name, La Fargeville. In the city of New York he acquired considerable real estate, including a hotel and a theatre, Tripler Hall, in which his son was later to witness the performances of Rachel and to make sketches of the great actress. The home of this resourceful, fortunate Frenchman, closely allied with the leaders amongst those of his countrymen whom political catastrophe had cast upon our shores and soon established in the friendliest relations with the quiet, old-fashioned society of New York, was naturally in the lower part of the town, where the dwellers in sedate houses preserving an aroma of colonial days regarded our present "up-town" as a sort of undiscovered country. It was in one of these houses, at No. 40 Beach Street, that John La Farge was born on March 31, 1835.

The scene of his birth was about mid-way between the Battery and Washington Square, within easy reach of both places. It lay under the shadow of one of our oldest churches, St. John's, and the North River was near at hand, the shore possessing, of course, a wholesome and picturesque character long since obliterated. Looking tenderly back at his earliest surroundings, and reconstructing in his mind's eye a peaceful, spacious neighborhood, La Farge writes, " We must always remember

that this is Old New York. The charm of St.
John's park extended to the entire length of
Beach Street, which lined it on the south." He
goes on to describe his first conscious vision
of it : —

" I had just come from Jefferson or Lewis
or any of those counties, where my father had
country places, and was selling his lands and
fighting the terrible Joseph Bonaparte for
damages owing to neglect and waste of tim-
ber. I had been taken as a treat to Watertown. I had seen wooden houses. I came by
night rides. I arrived in New York and came
into this street of brick houses, smothered in
the evening light, a scene of beauty which I
still have in my mind, and I sat on the steps
and entered into conversation with a little
negro boy, David, who was playing the jew's-
harp, which also was an absolute novelty to
me. I cannot to this day separate the houses
and the jew's-harp and my first sight of the
negro boy.

" He belonged to my uncle by marriage,
the Vicomte de la Barre de Nantueil, who
had just returned from selling his plantations.
Part of these, if I remember, he had from my
father, who rather hoped he would establish

himself in a country which was sure to bring
fortune, instead of returning to the narrow
life of the Norman or Breton gentleman (for
he was both) and to a struggle for a political
end which, of course, was not successful. My
uncle was a beautiful type of a certain moment
in France which cannot exist again. . . . He
was not a handsome man but evidently military. . . . He had served in Spain on the proper side and had with other gentlemen the
proper grades of service and had put down
the liberal reaction. He had tried the holding
of slaves and he hated it. Besides (though he
cared little for that, on account of his political
views) holding slaves withdrew the right of
citizenship from a Frenchman, according to
French law. Now he was also a very strict
Catholic and really a very religious man in a
simple, straightforward way. He had stood
godfather to the child of one of his slaves. According to church ideas he was responsible for
that child, so he brought David along with
him, with the intention of taking him to Europe and looking after him there, where he
would be free. Our law, of course, did not
recognize these points; in New York Davie
was a slave — and now comes in a touch of

serious comedy. The Abolitionists were after him, so that he had to be watched day and night, and this little nig wanted all the time to get out, as it was also his first town. They got him off, and then different tribulations fell upon my uncle. He had to put that boy into school, he even thought of college, but Davie was sure to fall in love and follow the travelling circuses and had to be brought back again. Then a trade was forced upon him and a little establishment in Paris (for my uncle thought it his duty) where he married, prettily, a young negro with the prestige of singularity and capital being a *trouvaille* in that sort of circle in Paris. And there, in 1856, I had the pleasure of calling upon him at his picture framer's shop, which was *my* small duty."

I must mention here the interesting fact of La Farge's clinging all his life to the region in which he first saw the light. In his youth the household shifted several times but never outside the boundaries of that "Old New York" he loved; and though there was a summer home at Glen Cove, Long Island, where the elder La Farge died, in 1858, the family life centred around the neighborhood of Washington Square. He would never desert it. He took a room in the Tenth Street studio building on his return from his first European travels, and down to the day of his death his various studios were there, with his stained glass workshops only a few blocks away, on the south side of Washington Square. He lived, too, with only very rare and brief departures to dwellings further north, within the same narrow radius. Clinton Place, Washington Place, Ninth Street, Tenth Street, lower Fifth Avenue, these were his landmarks for more than half a century. In fact, it was impossible to think of him as permanently established far from the spot where he had begun life as a thinking youth. The most distinguished of our old streets and our old houses made his natural background. Their atmosphere of dignified retirement from the sordid rush and pressure of a commercial city was his own atmosphere. It was, I think, one of the felicitous, most appropriate chances of his career that enabled him to place in the Church of the Ascension, at the corner of Fifth Avenue and Tenth Street, his finest mural decoration and some of the best of his windows. Fate was kind thus to permit him to enshrine his memory at the one

point in his native city with which his daily activities were so closely associated.

But we must rejoin him on the threshold.
He was born, as I have shown, into a family of
historic and romantic memories; but we take
leave for a moment of "battles long ago" and
their sinister rumble, and turn, rather, to some
domestic pictures of a reposeful simplicity. He
could clearly recollect his grandfather, Binsse
de Saint-Victor.

"He happened to have somewhat of an
artistic temperament," wrote La Farge; "it
was in the family; and he was as gentle and
amiable as his more celebrated brother, the
father of Paul de Saint-Victor, was not. My
grandfather took to painting miniatures and
giving drawing lessons and learned his art as
he went along. I dare say some of his miniatures may still exist. On a small scale he was
an exquisite painter. He was also a good
teacher and started me at six years old in
the traditions of the eighteenth century. My
grandmother, having married him, began a
school for young ladies."

Old Madame Binsse de Saint-Victor was,
one infers, a somewhat formidable but very
winning woman, whom La Farge recalled with

warm affection. Of her he draws this vivid
sketch: —

"My grandmother's school became extremely successful, her pupils being chosen
from among the aristocracy of New York, and
there I had the pleasure of falling in love for
the first time with Miss J., who at the age of
eighty sent me a few years ago her remem-
brances of that time. Besides the emotions of
love I had the advantage of knowing the emotions of jealousy, which are also an education.
When she was taken away and I felt that I
could no more see her put up her back hair, I
thought life had ended for me. I used occasionally to go to my grandmother's and follow some of the lessons. I was always severely
held up on French and I still have good eighteenth-century French as one of my possessions.

"My grandmother was very handsome,
with momentarily a somewhat severe expression, before which, I am sure, everybody bent.
Her ideas were of the eighteenth century and
somewhat opposed to the habits of the country.
Her occasional severity did not prevent my
grandmother from being both witty and liber-
ally forgiving in the way of literature. I re-

member, for instance, that she would discuss
La Fontaine and Boccaccio with my father
with full comprehension and great breadth of
view. She was not exactly pious but very religious, despising all meannesses and details of
worship but holding fast to the essentials of
belief."

All of La Farge's home influences bore in
one way or another upon the fostering of
moral principle but it amused him to recall the
very different lines along which these influences were exerted. The central government,
so to say, was strict, but it was in no wise rigid
in any bigoted sense. Side by side with the
ever-present law of the Roman Church there
were other kinds of admonition, though all
tended in the one salutary direction. Here are
some further glimpses of the spiritual elements
in his father's house: —

"At home I was not severely but strictly
trained in good English and fairly good be-
havior by an English governess who was
'High-Church,' the very highest of that early
date, who made me understand some details
of Anglican tradition. That was all very beautiful. Also, I had a little German influence. In
fact, my first prayer was 'Vater unser,' taught

me by my Alsatian nurse, who was brought
from the many Alsatians in my father's colony
in northern New York, for always, to his dy-
ing day, he had some form of Alsatian inheritance. I feel the advantage to this day of these
widely differing influences. My nurse's views
of religion and history were quite barbarous,
even to my childish knowledge, and I enjoyed
with a satirical pleasure her statements as to
the ignoble way in which Martin Luther and
his wife had been treated by the Pope at some
festival of food in common. Then she melted
out of my life."

Meanwhile, the retired soldier, who had
brought from his native Charente a certain
keen and rationalizing temperament, and had
learned in his European battles under Napoleon, as well as in his bitter experience at San
Domingo, to deal with life with a kind of imaginative practicality, played a notably steadying part in the training of his sensitive son. I
gather that La Farge's mystic vein, which he
never lost, was overlaid with sterner stuff
through his father's teaching, that the latter
drove at conduct, inculcating just the tangible
convictions needed to enrich and organize an
essentially religious nature. The tonic influ-

ence of the elder La Farge's way of dealing
with the lad is charmingly illustrated in this
recollection: —

"My father explained to me what right and
wrong was, according to his moral views,
which were extremely simple but very severe.
Nothing was more awful to him than lying or
equivocation. Several times I fell into the trap
of doing wrong, and one occasion, small as it
is, I think I shall register. We used to go together to see various French people down
town, and among others was a gentleman who
imported things from China. I knew that they
were not like our own Sèvres, and one day I
saw some little image and put it in my pocket
and by the time I got home I was in despair.
I had done a thing which was very bad, out
of mere want of thought. As soon as we got
home I told my father, thinking the world
would end then and there, but it did not."

He recalled other childish peccadilloes, as,
for example, writing an ambiguous letter ex-
cusing another boy for lateness at school, but
in his father's opinion he had not been so much
wrong as weak in the commission of this crime.
"I think I was a good boy," he says, and again
he describes himself as "very innocent." He

and his little comrades frolicked in the streets,
peppering with pea-shooters the pigs wander-
ing there, "and we said awful words which
we thought was swearing, the wickedness of
which we none of us very well understood."
I connect with these remote reminiscences a
conversation we had in the last year of his life
on questions of good and evil. There was a
wonderful gentleness in La Farge and though
he had gone through many a sharp passage
with contemporaries of his, and, like every man
of force and character, had had his enemies, he
could not feel in retrospect that he had ever
cherished injurious motives, that he had ever
had any predisposition toward wrong-doing.
It never occurred to him to see himself in the
rôle of "a plaster saint" but he knew that, on
the whole, he had been true to the spirit of
that far-away time in which the staunch French
moralists who brought him up had fixed him
in their faith.

"I suppose I went to school," he says in
his early recollections, but then he goes on
to speak of his reading as enjoyed under his
father's direction. His mentor "in a gentle
way, was firm and resolute," and he was glad,
besides, "to learn something of the innumer-

able pretty facts which mitigate the dryness
of geography and arithmetic, which I hated,
and which my grandfather insisted upon." It
was a household of exact thinking and strong
literary interests and evidently the boy had no
sooner learned his letters than he was encouraged to give himself to books. He speaks of
no nursery favorites. If he had them they were
abandoned at a precocious date. When he began to browse on veritable books he was given
sufficiently substantial fare, as witness this account:—

"On my sixth birthday I was presented
with a bookcase and a library and I sat down
to read 'Robinson Crusoe,' in a big illustrated
Harper edition with drawings by Grandville.
I never reread it until five years ago, at Newport, and the marvellous truthfulness of this
made-up narrative was forced upon me by my
own long life. In my library I had Voltaire's
'Life of Charles the Twelfth,' the 'Lettres à
Emilie,' 'Paul et Virginie,' 'Télémaque,' the
'Discours sur l'Histoire Universelle' of Bossuet, and Homer in a French translation, I
forget whose, but it was more enchanting than
'Robinson Crusoe.' Also the 'Swiss Family
Robinson' gave me notions of geography and

Wild Roses and Water Lily

natural history which I felt to be quite inadequate but very charming.

"On the other side the family bookcases were filled with the complete works of Voltaire and other long rows of eighteenth-century writers; there were the proper books of a French library, such as Molière, Corneille, and Racine, and then came the nineteenth century men, Paul Louis Courier, political and literary writers previous to 1830, and also all the military literature of that period. There were the proper English books of all the good men, and one beautiful copy of Byron, with the wonderful copperplates by Turner. On my father's table lay the New Testament in French, handsomely bound, with some pictures, into which he dipped from time to time. . . . Of course in my father's library there was a beautiful set of Balzac, with the famous illustrations of Tony Johannot, 'Don Quixote,' and ever so many contemporary engravings of the Napoleonic period; Napoleon with the King of Rome on his knee, the Empress Josephine, etc. Where, oh where, has gone the big lithographic portrait, nicely framed, of Henry the Fifth of France, which hung over my little bed, and for whom I had to say a

prayer every night and morning to please my
grandmother, who hoped I should one day help
the cause! My father, who held exactly oppo-
site opinions, would smile amiably, and sometimes said things which I did not understand.
Our whole family arrangements, intellectually, met every turn of politics, and my father
had seen so much and knew the reverse of so
many pages that it was easy for him to understand human variability."

La Farge himself, as I have previously indicated, was to share this comprehensive and
sympathetic outlook of his father's. In talk
about the history of his time little intimate
touches were constantly cropping out. Events
had faintly brushed him as they passed and
with others, dating from before his birth, he
had been made familiar not through books
alone. So clairvoyant a creature was certain to
receive clear and lasting impressions amongst
the actors in old dramas, rehearsing their ex-
ploits, even though, as he remarks in the foregoing passage, they said things which he did
not understand. His imagination would respond, though he had not yet obtained the
knowledge necessary to the coördination of all
that he heard. From my earliest acquaintance

with his memories of life under his father's
roof and the talk to which he then listened I
had always felt in him a curious magnetism,
the curious power to enthrall, which belongs
to the man who is in his proper person a link
with the historic past. Long after he had given
me, in a general way, this conviction of his
closeness to a vanished epoch and its heroes,
he sent me a letter containing a story which he
wished to have put in his biography. It illustrates in a very concrete form the stimulus he
drew from contact with his father's old friends.
Describing it as an incident in his early life,
"before I was twenty, or rather lasting up to
that through boyhood," he thus recites the
anecdote:—

"Our home had certain visitors who were
more distinctly private friends. One of them is
famous. Of course you have read Silvio Pellico, at least the 'Mie Prigioni.' Well, do you
remember his companion, Maroncelli, in that
awful dungeon of Spielburg, where they were
ten years, 1822 to 1832, underground, in a
small stone cell? Then the one-hundred-pound
chain began to mortify this good poet's leg and
they had to cut it off, and the indignant cry of
Europe got even as far as the German mind

and they were let out. Well, this one-legged man was a frequenter of our house, for my father, who was and had been more or less of a Carbonaro, liked him and they talked the politics more or less of the day, as far as Italy and its connections at least. And these were great, of course; Bonaparte and England, and Austria and Mazzini, and doubts about the justification of assassination, and the romance of Free Italy. But that also, as I remember, was wisely kept within some practical result. Every day the pressure on Europe was increasing; Napoleon III. was coming in and the boy, *me*, learned quite as much as the books and memoirs give to-day (from certain angles, of course). We did not know of Prussia, of course, yet. Prussia was to come in only with 1856–7–8, and our friends did not know — nor did Consul C. Lever, as you will remember, who wished to help Germany and Prussia in the interest of England!!! Read his journal, etc. I mean the novelist. To return to the good gray Poet. My memory of him tells me he was kind to his cruel tormentors and half murderers. He understood them; he understood the natural history of the gaoler, and would relate kindly the little cruelties inflicted in the small cell—underground and damp, stone wall, stone bench, nothing else—but even there the natural malignity of man found some way of expression."

In all that we have seen thus far of his childhood and youth we can trace forces working upon his moral nature, shaping his mind, giving an impetus to his curiosity about men and things, and incessantly feeding his imagination. There remains the appeal to his æsthetic instinct, the germination in him of the artist's passion. But it is important to note that there are none of the conventional stories to tell about a vocation proclaimed in infancy and persisted in against the obtuseness of unsympathetic elders. As a matter of fact, and as we shall see in detail later, it was to take La Farge a long time to find out that he was meant to be a painter and cared to be one. Where he had extraordinary good fortune was in breathing throughout his young impressionable years precisely the atmosphere needed to lay in his character a ground-work of good taste and to familiarize him with art without professionalizing it for him. He was in a position to take art as a matter of course, the best way in the world in which an artist can take it when he is young. The very envelope of his daily life was calculated to have some disciplinary and fruitful effect upon his ideas. "Our house was really very elegant," he says, "and suited my father, who had seen and lived in the proper kind of environment in Paris. The Napoleonic splendor had affected him without his knowing it, and most of our furniture was Empire." There was his grandfather Binsse de Saint-Victor, "painting miniatures and giving drawing lessons." The invitation of these conditions, coupled with the talk always going on around him, could not be withstood by the clever boy, even though the choice of the artistic career lay still very far in the distance before him. Everything conspired to prepare him for the path he was ultimately to follow. And it was characteristic of his good genius, considering his natural bent toward a wide, historic view of art, that it launched him under old-world auspices, so to say, starting him with sound anchors of judgment to windward.

Several years ago, in the summer of 1906, I had been asking him some questions about his work, and, when his health permitted, he set about answering them. Late that Fall he sent me from Newport a rich sheaf of mem-

ories, saying, "To note my beginnings in the
art of painting is a manner of writing an autobiography; and this I feel inclined to. It may
also serve to make correct the development
of my work, which is interesting to myself, at
least, and of course connects with the general
story of painting during the latter half of the
last century. It has been my fortune, whether
good or bad, — for nobody knows what the
real fortune is — it has been my fortune to
understand pretty well the direction, some of
the methods, the prejudices, the dislikes, the
admirations, of the schools of painting, especially of the French, a great deal over a century." The story of his experience, as he gave
it to me, goes back to those first years over
which we have already glanced: —

"The influences which I felt as a little boy
were those of the paintings and works of art
that surrounded me at home. Some reached
further back than the early Napoleonic period, the beginning of the nineteenth century.
There were on the walls a sea piece by Vernet; some imitation historical story, that of
Daniel, charming, however, in color, by Lemoyne; two great battle scenes, now ascribed
to Salvator; a large painting of Noah and his

sons, ascribed to Sebastiano del Piombo; some, indeed many, Dutch paintings of various authors and excellence, among them a beautiful Solomon Ruysdael which I yet see occasionally. All this and the very furniture and hangings of the Empire parlor did not belong to the Victorian epoch in which I was growing up.

"It so happened that my very first teachings were those of the eighteenth century and my training has covered almost a century and a half.

"I was just six years old and I had wished to learn to draw and paint for whatever was to come of it, a mere boy's wish. My father took me to my grandfather, the father of my mother, who had for some time been a painter, especially of miniatures, and not a bad one. I never knew exactly how he came by his training. I was too young to talk of such things; for as long as we are young, things merely happen; they don't come by any sequence. My grandfather had been obliged to do something for himself, on coming to the United States with wife and children, and his escape from San Domingo and the ruin of his plantation and wealth, for his plantation was one of the largest in the islands or on the mainland. He had

at that time, the end of our Revolution, received Admiral Rochambeau as a guest, and
my uncle, his eldest son, was named after the
Admiral. My grandfather had fled, like many
others, and was a ruined man. His slaves, of
course, were free and his plantation destroyed
and his mansion and all about it turned into a
wilderness. His fate was not solitary in that
moment of the world. . . . This has nothing to
do with my artistic education. I remember my
grandfather expressing a dislike to the insti-
tution of slavery. This came about through
something he said, which I vaguely remember, of his having gone to the coast of Africa
as a youngster, to get slaves; where he saw,
of course, some of the horrors of what was to
be the basis of his fortune.

"The old gentleman had fallen back on
this accomplishment and upon his general
reading, and he taught and painted and did
what was the evident thing, to use what had
been ornament for a basis of living. I ought to
add, however, that his studies had been serious enough to give him also a certain knowledge of architecture, so that he made designs for, and saw to the carrying out, of the
old French church in Canal street, which

was really a building of a good deal of character.

"To him, therefore, I came to get my first lessons of art, which were sadly prosaic and which would have driven me away if it had not been that my father insisted upon my carrying out anything that I had proposed to do. The teaching was as mechanical as it could be, and was rightly based upon the notion that a boy ought to be taught so as to know his *trade*. There was not the slightest alleviation and no suggestion of this being 'art.' After having learned thoroughly how to sharpen crayon, how to fasten paper, how to cover large surfaces with parallel lines so as to make a tint, I was gradually allowed to begin to copy things that represented something. I was given engravings to copy, which engravings were made on purpose to imitate the touch of the crayon. These were of older make than the lithograph, then only recently invented.

"Gradually the work became more interesting, and by the time I was eight years old I could begin to do something that had a certain amount of careful resemblance to an original. I still have some of these very early pieces of work. Then came more liberty and

I copied right and left, beginning even to paint in water color a little by myself. And the boy's little studies from nature have some amount of something, both in drawing and color.

"Of course, by the time that I was eight or ten the books of the house began to be unfolded to me, and the more modern works of that day, the forties, as shown in books, interested me very much. Already I was beginning to think that the samplers of my grandfather were rather stupid, which was what they were meant to be. Then came school, of course, and no more natural study of anything and even a hatred of the miserable teachings of the drawing master. Drawings of course were made to amuse the other boys or to kill time in the dreary hours that used to be the fate of the schoolboy at that time.

"Then, for a little while, broke a slight opening into the blue by my finding an English water color painter, who gave me thoroughly English lessons. At that time I was in the Grammar School of Columbia, which was very near to my teacher's rooms, so that I followed easily a discipline which would have been irksome with less chance of lounging.

But all this was absolutely inartistic at bottom, on my part, and nothing but the fancy of a youngster for something else than his usual occupation. Then came college, a still greater extinguisher of art, at least in the way of the use of the eye and hand.[1]

"Contrariwise, my professor in English took me suddenly into the literary and historical side of art. He was an Oxford man, had joined in the Oxford Movement, had become a Catholic with Newman and the others, and then a Catholic priest, further than which he could not go. We are talking of a date a few years after Newman's decision. Mr. Ruskin was beginning about this moment, 1851, perhaps, and his writings were a source of pleasure and instruction — I mean teaching — to my friendly professor. I was made or allowed to read anything which would bring up the beauty of the mediæval ideal, and even out-of-the-way knowledge was shown me, so that at this date I was already far away from the

[1] La Farge obtained his scholastic education from more than one source. Columbia, St. John's College at Fordham, and Mt. St. Mary's College at Emmitsburg, Maryland, all had a share in it. It was from Mt. St. Mary's that he was graduated, in 1853.

eighteenth century and was being taught how wrong all sorts of things in art were which did not agree with the mediæval. But all this was literature and history and archæology at bottom, rather than the study of art.

" Still, under such influences there was probably encouraged some more studious feeling. Perhaps the sight of some engravings of Albert Durer may have done something. But you must remember that at this time the photograph was only just beginning to be invented and really accurate copies of anything not in the fashion of the day were unknown. We do not realize sufficiently the enormous change of the early middle of this century in giving us, for the first time, a sense of responsibility in the copying of works of art of the past. The lithographs were beginning to help in that way and in a few years the photograph was to change the entire question. What one would have given at that time for a photograph from an old master such as we have by thousands every day, can hardly be guessed at. I remember how some years afterward M. Charles Blanc, Director of Fine Arts for France, sent me the first photograph taken from a fresco. Great treat, a wonderful success, etc.

"I was intending to state that to my great surprise to-day, the few serious drawings made by me at that date, in the very early fifties, are occasionally sufficiently good to look more respectable to me to-day than they did then, for I attach no importance to them except as study. But they were largely based on line and construction which, of course, gives a basis of seriousness.

"After college there was again a moment of a little interest in painting, because a French artist was an acquaintance of some French friends and needed lessons, so that several of us took some and I got into this distinct relation to the art of painting. Then came the acquaintance with pictures that were just showing their faces in this country, the French school of 1830. I remember the delight of buying a Diaz and a Troyon and a Barye for a few dollars that I had intended for books instead. The lithographs from these men beginning to be famous in Europe came into our market and affected many of us. Mr. Winslow Homer, whom I did not know until later, was a student of these things and has, like myself, been largely made by them.

"I knew few or no American painters,

though I was brought suddenly into the acquaintance of George Inness, who was beginning to turn from the American method, that I scarcely knew about, to the French. This was helped by my teacher, who had made his acquaintance and who was anxious to influence various of my acquaintances as buyers for the artist whose change of method, like the change of method of Mr. Homer Martin later, might involve him in that depreciation which artists have to risk in such cases. There is nothing the public detests more than a change in the manner of doing anything. We associate the man with his work to such an extent as to forget that, like everyone else, he may follow some path to suit himself.

"This acquaintance had very little influence upon me, because there were few chances of seeing our artist in his studio at his work, and my teacher, notwithstanding his admiration, was a person on a very small scale of capacity; the usual teacher that we know.[1] But the names he used became more and more familiar, especially as they were known to me through the literature which I was then absorbing.

[1] Note of 1910: "This is unjust. He became better."

"De Musset, Heine, and Balzac I had read every word of, as well as the greater part of the current writers of the day in France, and, of course, the Ruskinian explanation, connected with Turner, was a large factor in my training and my amusement. Acquaintances of mine, I should say friends, here in New York, had personally known these famous French writers. A few years later I was to meet some of the men of whom I had read or whose work I knew, though Balzac was to die in '51, and I was too late, in '56, on coming to Paris, to know more of Heine than that he had just died. Some of my new acquaintances and friends could tell me some few things more concerning the mysterious being who affected us all from his bed of pain and misery. All this literature is in absolute order with the influences of painting, for in France and in England the romantic leaven acted both in literature and in the other arts, even in the art of music."

The natural upshot of all this fermentation was a departure for Europe. With his horizon rapidly expanding it was inevitable that La Farge's gaze should turn abroad. He had the "seeing eye" and he was eager for new sensations. Again, however, we must remember that he still had no intention of adopting art as his profession. The spirit in which he started upon his travels is exactly defined in this fragment: "In the early part of 1856, April, I think, or March, I went to Europe, having already passed some little while in a lawyer's office — enough to make me doubt whether my calling lay in that direction, but the American habit, at least in these days, tended to place any doubtful mind into some such training or place of rest. Europe was to be a manner of amusement, and, for me, of taking up also some family connections." He embarked, by the way, in a famous old ship, "The Fulton," the then new side-wheeler about which everybody was talking. His father going with him one day, to look it over, told him that he had sailed the Hudson on the second trip of Fulton's boat. La Farge's objective point was, of course, Paris. His kinsfolk were there, the Saint-Victors, and, equally of course, as it seems to me when I consider on what a favorable stream his destiny was borne, they were the very friends to initiate him into *his* Europe.

III

EUROPE

IN Nadar's *portrait-charge* of Paul de Saint-Victor the celebrated man of letters carries himself in an attitude of superb aplomb, and with one hand nonchalantly sets off innumerable fireworks. Where are those fireworks now? Perhaps there are still readers who turn in leisurely browsings to his "Hommes et Dieux" or his "Femmes de Goethe," but as a literary personage the author of those once popular books, and of countless fugitive criticisms, long since ceased to rank amongst the salient figures in French prose. At the time of La Farge's first visit to Paris, to realize a cousinship which had always been kept alive by intimate communications between the two families, Saint-Victor, then in his thirties, was already a writer of some experience, and, in fact, was rising to the crest of the wave. He had been the secretary of Lamartine, but had turned journalist, and La Farge found him contributing articles on

The Three Kings

literature, art, and the theatre to half a dozen papers. Some years afterwards, to be exact, in 1870, he was to be appointed Inspector of Fine Arts and to take on the traits of maturity fitting in a governmental functionary, but in the 'fifties he was still young and exceedingly debonair, the true type of the *boulevardier* and *feuilletoniste*.

You hear a good deal about him in the "Journal" of the Goncourts, who report his vehement conversation, saturated in classical lore, but, for that matter, in the literature of all ages, and vitalized by an inexhaustible enthusiasm. They describe him in his own little salon, surrounded by facsimiles of the drawings of Raphael and other great Italian masters, and looking, himself, in a kind of radiant disorder, as handsome as an Ephebus of the Renaissance. They draw even more telling vignettes of their friend moving, to the manner born, through the glittering panorama of that amazing *monde* of Paris in which the ordinary aspects of a man's private life are pushed aside and almost obliterated by larger interests. Even the personal concerns of the successful *littérateur* of that day were part of the public spectacle. We see Saint-Victor at the Porte-Saint-Martin, looking on with a proprietary interest — and to the huge edification of scores of those who were in the secret — at the performance of Lia Felix, Rachel's sister, in a piece by Mocquard. As the Goncourts say, "La pièce n'est pas sur le théâtre, elle est dans la salle. L'intrigue et le drame, c'est la déclaration officielle des amours de Saint-Victor et de l'actrice en scène." All eyes were directed upon the marble face of the critic — when they were not turned toward the Ariadne he had abandoned, half hidden in one of the balconies behind an immense black fan. Talking about Rachel one night, La Farge showed me three little photographs of Lia, which had just come to light in some old bureau, and mused on the scenes they revived. He recalled the "family row" caused in Paris over the question of "recognizing" Lia's daughter and Paul's. Some of the kinsfolk did not like it. But ultimately Saint-Victor left his child all his money, a fact which I note as significant of his close identification with the romantic world in which he lived.

It was a feverish world, packed with work of an exciting sort, the work of the brain, dedicated wholly to ideals of art, and crowded

with brilliant personalities, all of whom were
Saint-Victor's comrades. Gautier, Gavarni,
Mario Uchard, About, Baudelaire, Flaubert,
Sainte-Beuve, were all of the company, forever doing great things and forever talking
about them at dinners, in the corridors of theatres, and at their favorite cafés. The conversation in Saint-Victor's circle took a wide
range. It soared to heights and not seldom it
was bowled as low as to the fiends. But whatever the issue these contestants in paradox
had gusto, ardor, a generous and enkindling
feeling for everything that led, or so much as
promised to lead, to a new thought, a new
emotion. It was a time of magnificent affir-
mations and Saint-Victor, letting himself go
when a thing excited his appreciation, never
erred on the side of understatement. Grant
Duff, in his diary, speaks of going with Renan
to visit Victor Hugo. "I found the old gentleman surrounded by his court," he says, and
Saint-Victor was amongst the acolytes. Loyalty to a romantic chief was characteristic of
him and a passage from his writings on Victor Hugo will give a good taste of his critical
quality. In his essay on "La Légende des
Siècles" he says:—

"In order to revive this buried world, the poet made for himself a new style, a tongue with a hundred chords, — Biblical, and Dantesque, feudal and popular, haughty and sincere, brilliant in tone, loaded with reliefs, streaked with the colors of life and the shifting shadows of dreamland, equally fit to paint a rose in bloom between the fingers of a child and a drunken carouse of brutes seated on a litter of corpses, to sing the *De Profundis* of a sphinx or the rollicking ballad of a band of sea adventurers. Since Dante and Shakespeare, no literature has produced its equal."

His friends praised his style and he is remembered for that, if for nothing else. To-day it seems perhaps a little florid, unduly charged with romantic fervor. And even in his own time he had his critics. Edouard Grenier records a suggestive saying of Lamartine. "As for Saint-Victor, he declared that you could not read his works without blue spectacles."

I do not believe that La Farge put them on. He was twenty-one and keen upon the fray. If anything had been needed to make it rose-colored for him it was just his reception into a group of people whose way of life, at some points at least, coincided with that which he had left behind him. The strangeness of Europe was instantly modified, if not completely dissipated, by a consciousness of his being merely in another home. He told me that he had often regretted not asking more questions in those days, though asking questions was one of his foibles. "I was too young," he said, "too young and light-headed and happy." Once more I must recur to his imagination, wax to receive and marble to retain impressions little by little deepening that insight of his into human problems which was one of the great resources of his life. His father had accustomed him to an atmosphere full of the meaning of history and in Paris he drew nearer to the Napoleonic drama. This and his quick apprehension of character made him a delighted frequenter not only of the Bohemia in which his cousin moved but of his grand-uncle's salon, where memories of an heroic past were still fresh and bleeding.

Paul de Saint-Victor, like his American relative, had a notable parent, an old lion of a man who "had lived a violent life in the time of the Revolution." He had translated Anacreon and had artistic predilections, but these elements of a delicate charm were subordinate to the sterner appeal that he made. "He had seen every execution except that of the Queen, and he crossed Charlotte Corday as she came down the steps of Marat's house, into which he was going to see his publisher, who lived in the same building. It may be that my granduncle, who at that time was politically a very religious agent for the throne and the crown, only later to fall under de Maistre's guidance, was going upstairs to see about some of his lighter works, which, I do not know. A certain fondness for the stage and its ladies brought him later, in 1805, against Stendhal in the person of a Mlle. ———, who preferred Saint-Victor." The lady was Melanie Guilbert, an actress who figures at length both in the "Journal" of Stendhal and in his "Correspondance." In the former the jealous lover scornfully dubs his rival a poetaster but it is plain that Saint-Victor caused him endless worry. One can imagine with what breathless attention La Farge drank in the reminiscences of this veteran, in the intervals of exploring Parisian society with the young leaders in art and letters.

As he looked back in after days upon the

" Noli Me Tangere "

European opportunities of his youth he was
wont to regret, as I have just indicated, that
he had not taken better advantage of them.
But he knew that those old encounters had
not been wasted upon him and he gives them
their full value in the narrative of his artistic
education, which we here resume:

"My granduncle, whose house I used to
frequent in Paris, had been a writer upon art,
a collector of fine paintings, and acquainted
with many famous artists of his prime. He
had also known most of the literary men who
could have come within his chances. . . . My
granduncle had also a further spread to his interests and consequent connections; he had
been a fervent Royalist, engaged in all sorts
of difficulties during the Revolutionary and
Napoleonic periods. Like many others he had
become a strong churchman and in his forced
exile in Russia had known the great type of
his efforts in that way, the famous de Maistre.
So art and literature were there at my hand,
in rather an ancient form, but with the charm
of the past, the eighteenth century and the
wonderful beginning of the nineteenth.

"Occasionally men like my granduncle
were troubled because their friends of reli-

gious literary views, even Royalists besides, were beginning to uncover more and more the merits of the mediæval painters and the glories of mediæval art. For the younger men as typified in England by Mr. Ruskin and some earlier ones all this was natural enough, but in France the conservative feeling was shocked by the new admirations which had not belonged to their early days and which often gathered strength from their own principles of philosophy and religion. We do not realize to-day the contradictory currents which must have tortured the high thinking people of the end of the middle of the last century.

"To me, of course, this was a delightful source of pleasure. To have my granduncle refer to David and Guérin as the normal students, though without depreciating the merits of the less severe artists of the eighteenth century; to have him speak of Ingres, then almost at the height of his power, as a person a little too much tinged with sentiment, as a master *not sufficiently strict*, was allowing me to enter into the minds of my predecessors as far back as his own reached, and in all my thinking since then, I have valued beyond everything this knowledge of the manner of looking at things of a generation so far back. I feel as if I had lived, myself, back this hundred years or more, in the minds of these few people who kept up for my youth this training and these sentiments of an earlier day.

"Contrariwise, and most curiously, my granduncle's son, my cousin, Paul de Saint-Victor, was a brilliant, fashionable, successful writer upon art of all kinds, from the theatre, through all literature, to painting and to drawing, and his criticisms were all important then. Even to-day they have a certain merit, though, like all momentary writings, some of their best value has passed. Quite in opposition to the views of his father, my cousin stood by and defended the new men, more or less; at any rate those especially of whom my granduncle was, if I may say so, afraid. As you know, perhaps, through writings of that day and this, my cousin was intimate with some of the best-known writers, as, for instance, Gautier, so that all these names, and occasionally themselves, came up to explain and interest one in the art and the literature that was passing away and in that which was coming up.

"I was taken to see the remarkable work of a promising young artist, called Gérôme. I heard rumors of almost all, except one of whom I was to learn a great deal later; that was Millet, whose name never came up. But of course there was a constant war and great abyss between the two ends of French art, that represented by M. Ingres or M. Gérôme, and that of my friends the painters of twenty years before. In one place, however, there was an attempt at bringing these extremities together. That was at the house of Chassériau, the artist who was to die that very year (if I remember), but who was apparently at that time a healthy man, doing a great deal already 'classed,' as the French call it, so that whatever he thought was of importance. You know him either well or not at all or very little, because he has left so little. But if you remember him you will remember those beautiful portraits of his sisters, which made one of the marked paintings in the Centennial Exposition of the great Paris show in 1900. They are finer than the semi-classical painting of the Tepidarium, which is far from having to-day the importance which it had when I was there. What he was doing then has been, I suppose, almost destroyed in the disasters of the Commune. I say almost, because a few years ago there were remains. Those are the paintings decorating what is called, or used to be called, the Cour des Comptes.

"These paintings are to me of extraordinary importance as reconciling the schools which he valued and as making the future of a person at that time quite unknown, and, in fact, not yet a character in art; that is Puvis de Chavannes, who succeeded to a great deal of Chassériau's ideas and training and in fact, to more than that, to the drawings and studies and the personal friendships of this man whom I used to go and see. Another person who I think was influenced by him was Moreau. I mean the man whose museum of paintings has been lately opened to all, while so much of his work remained a closed book even to many art lovers.

"At Chassériau's the war raged all the time. At once one was asked what one held in regard to M. Ingres or M. Delacroix, for the head of the house had been a favorite pupil of Ingres, a promise of the right academic future, and then had been converted suddenly, like Paul, to Delacroix, for whom he professed, rightly, an extraordinary admiration. I may regret to-day that neither through him nor my cousin, nor my uncle, nor any social connection, I saw the great man whose works I knew about beforehand, through literature, especially, and whose astounding paintings had been, with those of the old masters, one of the first great sensations of my first days in Paris. But I was then and I am yet, averse to knowing famous people, nor could I, at that date, have obtained from the great man any real value. That I also appreciated. Hero worship is not an educational basis. I doubt if, with a person of that importance, there would have been anything to learn until one had attained already a sufficient capacity to absorb or discuss. So that my regret is merely a sentimental one, as it is in regard to many others whom I either accidentally or on purpose neglected meeting.

"I was told last year, by Sir Martin Conway, that I had done wrong through not using later my introductions to Mr. Ruskin, because he was so amiable, but I have not the slightest doubt of my having been right. We should certainly have disagreed if there had been any discussion. At that later time, also, 1872–3,

Mr. Ruskin was especially aggravating — to such an extent that Burne-Jones, a special pet of his, told me that he had given up reading anything by him. (This is a memory of much later, some nearly twenty years. At the time I am speaking of, there was no B-J.)

"As I have explained, my studies or my impressions would to-day be called literary. They were so to a certain extent but more than anything else they were archæological. Travelling somewhat in France, to make the acquaintance of relatives in out of the way places, I became naturally interested in learning by eyesight the things that I had read about mediæval architecture and mediæval art especially, because a previous enthusiasm had been fostered at home. The acquaintance of a few archæologists in out of the way places was favorable also. In Paris, on the contrary, my few acquaintances at the time were classical scholars.

"The churches brought me to the knowledge of ancient glass and I was able to use, for understanding it, what I had read in the writings of the illustrious Chevreul. He had explained more especially, years before, the points of ancient work in glass and then he had written, as you know, and perhaps was writing, on the optical views of color. This reading determined, I suppose, more than anything else, the direction which my painting took some years afterward, when I began to paint. People like myself were laughed at in those days, even by scientific men. Later, of course, the question was to become one of the most important in the work of the modern Frenchmen. Much later I was to use these principles and theories when I took to working in glass, and I am still surprised that no one that I know of has worked in the same way therein. My impression is that Chevreul's teachings in regard to ancient glass are as far back as the thirties.

" About my time Viollet-le-Duc was writing and teaching and influencing many people, but I was out of his line of acquaintance and only began to know him on my return home. The mediæval art that he explained and recommended would not have appealed to me through his own work and buildings, and I am glad that I did not at that time suffer from what later annoyed me through his interpretations of the past. On the contrary, just then, through a tour in Belgium, I was able to see

some of the painting which we may call
mediæval and which begins modern art, and I
was, as was right, steeped in admiration. The
few little drawings that I made I still keep
as fair and creditable notes, few as they are.
They show to me that I had a passable understanding of the beautiful things that I admired.

"All this led me to a desire to understand
the mechanical methods of the early painters,
especially those who invented the modern art
of painting in oils, and by some chance of
good fortune I made the acquaintance, in
Brussels, of Henry Le Strange, who you know
decorated Ely Cathedral. He was interested
in me and in what he had to tell me practically
about manners of painting. I learned from
him about painting in wax, for instance, and
was led to read various documents of information with regard to that question of the early
ways of painting."

At this point, approaching the subject of
La Farge's brief stay in the atelier of Couture,
a letter of his to Miss Barnes supplies a passage of high importance. Nothing is more interesting in the psychology of La Farge than
the slow and even unpremeditated fashion in

which he drifted into his vocation. Vaguely
he seems to have known his powers, yet to
have remained indifferent and uncertain before the gate which he had only to open in
order to pass to a happiness that he came to
regard as one of the most blessed gifts of the
gods. Writing to Miss Barnes of the choice
gently forced upon him in Paris, in 1856, he
says : —

"At some time or other during that year,
when, I cannot remember, my father (through
my mother, I think, so that I have never
known what he really thought) advised me
to study painting, of which I was rather fond,
on the ground — which was quite certain —
that I was wasting my time and I think with
a faint suggestion, not to me but to the family
mind, that perhaps I was living in a little
faster way than their habits accepted; which
in reality was perfect 'rot.' I was like all
other young men, but, differently from many
other young men, I was enormously interested in everything except strict science and
the mathematical side of knowledge. I was
always very anxious to please my father as
a matter of sentiment, and very willing to go
and learn the practice of painting, about which

Christ and Nicodemus

I used to hear a great deal, because a great deal of my time was spent with people whose pleasures and interests were literary and artistic."

How he decided to enter a particular studio, and in what mood he took up his task there, he goes on to tell in the narrative upon which I have already drawn : —

"My American acquaintances were then very much inclined to the painter Couture, who had quite a number of Americans in his studio and had been the master of several of them, well known in Paris and having quite a position of their own. One of these, Edward May, took me to the master one day and I explained to him what I wished, which was to get a practical knowledge of painting, as practiced by him. I also made him understand that I was doing this as a study of art in general and had no intention of becoming a painter. This he at first thought preposterous and was probably somewhat astonished at the youngster who laid out this programme in such an unusual manner. But I argued with him, and won his good graces, so that the next day in the early morning I entered the studio and took my place with the others. I was given, in the usual manner, by the student in control, a seat and place, paper, etc., and I began drawing from the model before me. There being no one to guide me, and feeling that the way the others drew was not mine, I went on my own way.

"That day or next came in the great man, who, instead of objecting to my work having so little in common with those following his system, was pleased to say, on the contrary, that mine was the only one that really gave the motion of the model. To-day, when I look at the drawing, I can see why the master recognized something in the work of the boy which had a value of its own. He told me to go ahead and that the others 'tried to be little Coutures, as if a little Couture was worth anything.'

"I was impatient to paint according to school ways, for which I had come, but the routine of the school demanded drawing in the Couture way, and as I unfolded my plan to him he thought I might wait till the next year, and meanwhile go on studying the variations of drawing by the old masters, many of which, as you know, are in the Louvre. This I did for a time, returning occasionally to the studio.

On the whole, I did not stay there more than a couple of weeks."

Before leaving this episode in his career I must rescue from a talk of ours an interesting souvenir of his stay with Couture. Puvis came in one day, wanting a model, and he chose La Farge. "Perhaps," he said to me, "it was something in my face. I don't know what I posed for. Some study, perhaps. It would be amusing to discover myself somewhere in his works, if one could look them over in a lot of photographs." Released from obligations which, as we have seen, he had only lightly assumed, as it were in passing, he set forth upon his travels. Speaking of the copies of drawings by the old masters which he made at Munich and Dresden, he continues : —

" These copies have some of the qualities of the originals, showing that at that time I had become sensitive to the differences of the artists. You must remember that there were no photographs and that one had to travel, as I did, many hundreds of miles and many days' journey to find these things of which, now, we have duplicates in our portfolios. Study of the drawings of the old masters seemed to me a logical method of learning and learning very seriously. If I copied the painting for which the drawing had been made I could only copy the surface, without knowing exactly how the master had made this result. But I knew that in the master's drawings and studies for a given work I met him intimately, saw into his mind, and learned his intentions and his character, and what was great and what was deficient.

"Meanwhile, thereby, I kept in touch with that greatest of all characters of art, style, not the style of the Academy or of any one man, but the style of all the schools, the manner of looking at art which is common to all important personalities, however fluctuating its form may be.

"In Denmark, besides making the acquaintance of some of the painters, I made some studies in the Copenhagen gallery. Among others I made a fairly careful study of the Rembrandt there, the 'Supper at Emmaus.' I had plenty of time to do it in. The summer days are endless. I was alone and the guardians treated me as a spoiled child, bringing me lunch and allowing me to sponge out the surfaces of the great master, whose work, fortunately, had not been varnished or retouched.

As I did not consider that I knew enough about oils to copy anything of importance, I painted in water color, in the English way, as I had been taught. I was enabled to learn a great deal of the methods of Rembrandt and to connect them with my studies, outside of any idea of practice as yet. I have lately recovered this water color, which had been lost for many years. It came back to me just fifty years after I had finished it, and I had finished it on the anniversary of the birth of Rembrandt, two hundred years before.

"Rubens I followed in Belgium, later, trying to see every painting of his throughout the whole kingdom; and as many of his pupils as I could gather in. As far as having seen the master's work, I can say that I have seen the greater mass of it. I made no studies; in fact Rubens is not one to work from easily, nor would it have been available for me to imitate, without a great knowledge of painting, the tremendous flow of color and light so gloriously spread over that enormous space of painted surface, either all his own or that of his pupils also. One thing I felt to be astonishing, because I had not thought it out, and that was, how beautifully the work of Rubens con-

nected with the early mediæval paintings that
I so much admired. And yet one might suppose the greatest difference between the delicacy and the closeness of the study of the
older men, their reticence and their care, and
the apparently reckless ease of the last great
Fleming. But I learned how careful in reality
was this generous abandonment to energy,
how the first preparation determined the future; and how prudent that first preparation
was.

"I did not return to Couture's. I do not
know what I should have done had I remained
in Europe and in Paris. But I did not admire
his work or his views of art and he annoyed
me, notwithstanding his friendliness, by his
constant running down of other artists greater
than himself. Delacroix and Rousseau were
special objects of insult or depreciation. He
never referred to Millet, for whom some of
his best pupils, among others, William Hunt,
had left him — a fact which he never forgave,
as I learned later. I mention my indifference
to my master, which was more than indifference, all the more because it is not usual. Let
me add that I was not the only one. Among
others, I take it that Puvis, whom we saw once

or twice there, must have felt that way. Some
of his first work, even that announcing his
future powers, has some mark of Couture's
methods. I suppose that it is almost impossible for a serious mind to pass through some
painter's studio without getting a little of his
method or manner or something, if it is worth
while. I take it that that is one of the charms
of the Italians and also that we would realize
the cause better if we knew more of their
actual lives. Some of the things that catch are
purely mechanical, but as the art of painting is
a mechanism, that mechanical influence is an
important one. The Japanese have that thoroughly in their identifying the school with the
shape of the brush.

"Whatever I wished or intended or thought
of was put aside by my return home, determined by my father's wishing me back on account of his illness. I returned in the winter of
1857–8, having spent a part of the autumn in
England on my way home. I had plenty of
time to give to looking at paintings, because
almost every one for whom I had letters was
away from London. After a little while I went
to Manchester and spent several weeks at the
great Exposition, which was the first of the

special exhibitions of paintings collected from private and royal galleries. It is still remembered as the 'Manchester Exhibition' and is one of the turning points of the public's acquaintance with the art of many countries. As you know, the wealthy collections of England were poured into the great show, and certainly the pleasure of seeing, side by side, the great Titian and the great Velasquez and the great Rubens in all their contradiction, was an education for any intelligent and sympathetic mind. We saw there the Velasquez, the figure of the woman lately bought for the National Gallery. It had come out of the shade and went back to it these fifty years. But I am pleased to think that my little memorandum sketch has some recognition of it, however careless.

"But besides the miles of old masters, there were some of the quite new; the pre-Raphaelites, whom I knew of by reading and by some prints but whom now I could see carefully. They made a very great and important impression upon me, which later influenced me in my first work when I began to paint. But of that I had no warning."

It was still without any warning in a broader

sense, without presage of the ambitions that were soon to burn in his breast and the achievements to which he was to push forward, that he took ship and returned to America.

IV

THE EVOLUTION OF AN
ARTIST

IF there is one thing more than another
which I hope has been made plain in the
preceding chapter it is that none of La Farge's
experiences abroad had crystallized his ideas
of art into a formula. Europe had not fitted
him out with a technique. It had awakened in
him, and to some extent had organized, a habit
of mind. Potent influences were singing in his
head like wine. He could not return unscathed
from his contact with the impetuous adherents
of the romantic movement. But he was committed to nothing, neither to the "rectitude"
of Ingres nor to the prodigal method of that
master's abhorred rival, neither to the flat-
brush trick of the Salon and the gray light of
that official tabernacle, nor to the freer atmosphere which the Barbizon men were carrying into vogue. He was, instead, in the mood
to think it all over.

Anatole France has a saying on Gavarni
which is absolutely applicable to La Farge:

John La Farge in 1885

"He thinks, and that is a cause of wonder in the midst of all this world of artists who are content with seeing and feeling." The point is one of the greatest importance, to be kept constantly in mind; and we have at the same time to recognize the equilibrium established in his artistic nature. That he thought much did not prevent his seeing and feeling. It acted both as a check and as a fertilizing influence; it stayed his hand from relapsing into routine, and, always unfolding to him new phenomena in the worlds of nature and art, spurred him to redoubled efforts. The duality of his genius is sharply expressed in some of his remarks to me. "Were it not for our learning by instinct and not by thought we should never do anything. . . . Painting is, more than people think, a question of brains. A really intelligent man would not have to *see*, if he could only find his place, any more than a musician is obliged to hear the music he writes. Of course the actual execution modifies the more intellectual view within which the artist works." Yet he knew as well as any painter that ever lived the transcendent necessity of purely visual operations. Once, when he was anxious about the completion of a decoration and the securing of some proper place in which to exhibit it, he wrote to me: " My studios are too small to be quite certain of the effect of the work at a distance. I mean by that that it is more prudent to go by one's eye rather than by reasoning, which, so far, I have to work with." But where many a painter thinks that it is enough "to go by one's eye," La Farge took that for granted, as one of the rudimentary truths, and, steeping himself in reflection, brought all manner of constructive thought to the development of his work.

He was the most assiduous experimentalist in art that we have ever had. He came back from Europe a student and in 1903, when he inaugurated the Scammon lectures at the Art Institute of Chicago, he began by saying to the budding artists in his audience, "Notwithstanding my greater age, I am still a student." Letters written in his last illness beautifully illustrate the joyous, almost boyish, zest with which he had always talked to me of his interest in pigments and processes. "I had a bad yesterday and night and morning to-day," he writes. "It's all I can do to hold on." But even then he was busying himself over the cataloguing of nearly a hundred water colors

that were going off to an exhibition in Boston,
and, with his accustomed buoyancy, lifting
him above ill health to the things he loved, he
goes on to say, "In all these things of misery
I have had a great consolation. I have found
the Japanese and Chinese paints chosen for
me by Okakura some years ago—all, of
course, of great purity and of long tradition.
Such a 'Kano' blue! The exact Chinese ver-
milion of the extremest best! This is not
necessary but it may help if I live,—and it is
especially valuable as a superstition, because it
looks as if luck smiled a moment through the
clouds. The colors of A. D. 812, of A. D.
1340!"

Another letter, written at the same time,
shows him struggling under the same burden
but again losing himself in his art, and pausing,
too, in spite of pain, to philosophize:—

"I am working very hard at 'finishing'
some water colors. . . . It is very hard work.
Two or three are important, perhaps good.
The rest, I hope, are amusing. There are
some experiments among them, because I
have found that when I was ill and could not,
or thought I could not, go about or get on my
steps before my painting, I would sit and do

little things in size. For me many of them
are my best work, as they are for everybody.

" Have you ever seen my reconstitution of
Chinese painting? I defy a Chinaman to deny
that I have used correctly his basis. Of course
I can't work his technique and be *honest*, nor
can I even quite use some of the things I most
admire in him—let us say his 'color,' for instance. I have to be true to 'us'— paint or
draw with the knowledge of the world. Any
one who is a 'primitive' to-day is in so far a
fraud. But then, fortunately, those games are
not the games of the better men, who are glad
to be free and not imitative. And that, you
know, can be done even within the enclosure
of a 'school,' or the following more or less of
a beloved master. Chassériau used to tell me
that it was good to leave a cherished method
behind one and sail into the blue, as he did
after Delacroix, pursued by Ingres' maledic-
tions. Like the story of Theseus and Ariadne.
But for a very sick man I write too much. A
bientot, I hope."

I remember his appreciation of Dupré's de-
finition of art, as the expression of the painter's reverence and admiration for what he sees
in nature. "It is never," he added, "the *mere*

representation of what we see." The ideal he believed in, and followed in his practice, was that which he describes in "An Artist's Letters from Japan," in that tribute which he pays to the Oriental craftsman lavishing all that is in him upon the execution of a little *netsuke* or *inro*. "And when he has finished, — because to do more or less would not be to finish it, — he has given me, besides the excellency of what we call workmanship, which he must give me because that is the bargain between us — he has given me his desires, his memories, his pleasures, his dreams, all the little occurrences of so much life." Elsewhere, in one of the lectures going to form his "Considerations on Painting," he develops the same point and gives it a certain autobiographical turn. "After all," he says, "remember that what I tell you is the result of life, whether in thought or in action; and that I am only able to give principles and foundations for thinking, through having visited certain regions of thought, through surprises that have fallen upon me, and that what confidence I have today in talking to you is based on no *a priori* certainty that I had it all before beginning."

These numerous citations are made, of

course, with but one purpose, to expose La
Farge's point of view. The point of view is
everything, and, in the case of a genius so
complex as his, no evidence is too slight, too
fugitive, to serve us. Moreover, knowledge
of the breadth of view which governed all his
artistic proceedings supplies us with a touch-
stone especially desirable at the present time,
when the student has to be on his guard against
the oracles toward whom he would naturally
turn for guidance. There are some painters,
very clever painters, too, who can sink to well-
nigh fathomless depths of fatuity on the subject of what constitutes the art of painting. It
is easy to understand how they have fallen into
a rather circumscribed way of thinking on that
subject. Thirty odd years ago, when the mi-
gration of our young artists to Paris had set
in, but the public taste for the painted anecdote had not abated, the returned American
found himself placed more or less on the defensive; and, often without knowing it, he has
been on the defensive ever since. Commended
by his French master for a well-managed passage in technique, he came back defiantly to
flaunt his manual dexterity in the faces of the
collectors, who were then clinging with pious

faith to the "Kiss Mummy" picture. He has not only gone on painting the *morceau* but has settled down to the touching belief that there is something talismanic about it. There is something talismanic about it, in the right hands, when the instinct for beauty and for style is so strong that it raises technique to a higher power. La Farge himself has a good saying to stiffen the back of the painter who will listen to nothing that seems even faintly to disparage the purely technical function. "The touch of the brush is so difficult when it comes to be a very successful thing, that it becomes ennobled." But this is a very different thing from making a fetish of *facture*.

La Farge knew all about *facture*. No other man of his time knew more. All his life long he was interested in its problems and it is suggestive to see how, in his dealings with the old masters, he puts his finger on whatever prefigurements they disclose of our modern connoisseurship in technique. In his essay on Raphael, coming to treat of "The Mass of Bolsena," he calls the reader's attention to the portrait of Pope Julius, "painted with the apparent velocity and ease which we credit to such a man as Velasquez," and he used to say that when he had sat at the feet of Rembrandt, copying the "Supper at Emmaus," in Copenhagen, he received a technical lesson that had never ceased to affect his practice. What he would have repudiated with vigor would have been the assertion that Rembrandt, or any other single master, could have taught him the whole duty of the artist, and, conversely, it was impossible for him dogmatically to assert that any given mode was wrong. In fact, he regarded such assertion with an amused tolerance, feeling a little sorry for those who made it a habit, and assuming, in kindly fashion, that by and by they would grow out of their provincialism. There were so many ways of caressing the surface of a painting! When I mentioned to him the discovery of an accomplished young painter that Fra Angelico did not know how to paint, it greatly tickled him and he recalled the similar remark made by a junior of his, full of Impressionism and the like, when they were standing in the Louvre before a picture by the devout Florentine. "I wondered," he said, "how my young companion would have gone to work to get just the blue of that robe, just the white of that wall, and to draw just that line against the background." There was no answer to his questions, "and," he added to me, "I have often wondered how I myself could have done those things." He was full of wonder when he came back from Europe in his youth. For the manner in which he gradually solved his problem we turn again to his own narrative.

"I knew that on my return I should go back to reading law; which I accordingly did, though stealing as much time as I could for visits to some of my new friends, the painters and architects. They made a manner of link with Europe, at least the architects did, Richard Hunt and his two or three students, George Post and Van Brunt, and William Ware and Richard Gambrill.

"I only touched the merest corners of what was being done. I did not know of our pre-Raphaelites here, as a body, though I spent some time with Stillman, who was one of their prophets. I knew Boughton, who was to leave us soon, and a few of the Hudson River men.

"In the middle of the next year I began to be a little freer of myself; I saw a little more of the few artists, and even took a room at the Studio Building in Tenth Street, where occasionally I made some little drawings, and even tried to paint on a small and amateurish scale, but I recognized that I needed a training in the practice of painting. I had even thought of going back again to Europe to go through a certain discipline, which if not absolutely necessary is still valuable. It is preferable to have very good teaching and the best, but even a poor one in such a mechanical art has enormous value.

" Talking of this one day to Richard Hunt, merely because his French training had made him acquainted with and respectful of the artists of France whom I especially liked, he suggested that I might like to be with his brother, William, who thought of taking some pupils, who was settled in Newport, and with whom I could continue the practical teachings that I had almost begun at Couture's studio; Hunt being, of course, a favorite and brilliant pupil of Couture's. I met thereupon Bill Hunt, saw some piece of his work, and was pleased both with the man and with what he did and said, and with all of that very charming character, so that in the spring of 1859 I came to Newport to try the experiment, and began in a little more serious way than before.

"But a disappointment was in store for me, and it was this, — that Hunt had abandoned the practice of Couture, which was what I wished to continue. He was then arranging, as men often do, other influences to suit his previous ones and was painting in a manner which, however interesting to me, was not what I had come to get. But his general influence was so good, and the pleasure of devoting almost all my time to painting as a task under a teacher, kept me satisfied with my momentary position. And there was always something to learn from a new man whom I liked, to learn or to share with him, for we found more and more common admirations. He introduced me to the knowledge of the works of Millet, of which he had many, including the famous 'Sower,' and very many drawings, and more especially to the teachings, the sayings, and the curious spiritual life which a great artist like Millet opens to his devotees. Every day some remark of Millet's was quoted, some way of his was noticed, some part of his life was told; he was, in this way, in those studios, a patron saint.

"Notwithstanding, though I even copied a Millet or two, I was firmly resolved against

following him either with or without Hunt, in
the methods which were especially developed
by the great Frenchman. His previous methods, which one sees more distinctly in some
of his landscapes, and, of course, in his early
work, were nearer what I had been looking
for, however less poetic and more commonplace they might be, but my aim was study
and the acquaintance with methods of work
that would connect generally with the past,
not with new formulæ which were abridg-
ments. So that to some extent I had to fight
out my own issue, and Hunt and I disagreed,
but we had so many common beliefs and
Hunt's was so charming a mind, that often he
was the first and only one to praise me when
I departed from his method, as from his general views.

"All this refers to landscape more particularly, because the closed light of the studio is
more the same for every one, and for all day,
and its problems, however important, are extremely narrow, compared with those of out
of doors. There I wished to apply principles
of light and color of which I had learned a
little. I wished my studies from nature to indicate something of this, to be free from *re-*

cipes, as far as possible, and to indicate very carefully, in every part, the exact time of day and circumstances of light. This of course is the most ambitious of all possible ideas, and though attempted to some extent through several centuries from time to time it is only recently that all the problems have been stated, in intention at least, by modern painting.

"In a certain way Hunt recognized the value of the ideas and the value of their result, but his aim was quite the other way; and that was to find the recipe which would be sufficient for noting what he wished to do. Herein he was following the steps of Millet, but as Millet himself objected to him, "That is all very good, but what have you *got to say* with it?" This is not to say that Hunt had not a right to do whatever he wished in such a way, especially as for him in general the future was merely as the past in representing figures and portraits, and he gave up the entire question of the place in which the figures lived, air and light and space. We used to talk, however, about it all.

"To recall all these discussions would be a lengthy matter, but it is necessary to indicate

this great divergence of point of view. We
had, of course, certain previous teachings in
common and certain mechanisms. We used
similar paints, and canvas which I imported;
we made a shadow of flesh in the same way
occasionally and we used the same brushes.
We also used similar grounds to paint on, until
I began to change according to circumstances.
In fact, I suggested to Hunt the preparing of
his paintings in a way that he had not so far
practiced, and I occasionally helped him in one
or two of these preparations, as did some of
his other pupils.

"I, too, the next year, began to paint in a
different way according to this notion, a very
elementary one. But the main practical point
in which we differed was this, which serves as
a type or note of diversity: Hunt thought it
useless to carry the refinement of tone and
color to the extent which I aimed at in my
studies, telling me that there would not be one
in a hundred or five hundred artists capable of
appreciating such differences of accuracy —
their eyes and their training would not be sufficient. This objection seemed to me, as I told
him, exactly the reason why I should, for certain, aim at these variations from *recipe*. So

much the better, if only one man in a thousand could see it; I should then have exactly what I wanted in the appeal to the man who knew and to the mind like mine.

"The first and special work I did according to my liking was in a few months after coming to Hunt. The first distinctive paintings were a couple of landscapes painted in December, 1859, and perhaps as late as January, 1860. They still remain and you can see one of them at Mrs. Gardner's and one at Sir William Van Horne's. They are each studies out of the window to give the effect and appearance of *looking out* of the window and our not being in the same light as the landscape. And also to indicate very exactly the time of day and the exact condition of the light in the sky. This to be done without using the methods of mere light and dark, and thus throwing away the studio practice for any previous habit.

"This, of course, is contrary to most of the manners of making studies, though to-day it would be better understood than it could have been then. I note that I had then, and have no objection now, and much admiration, for the reverse way of doing, and of using a conventional method. Of course that would be if the

thing were beautiful and in some relation, as,
for instance, Millet's later work, while his
early work was more in the meaning of my
studies. Therein and in the work I did during
my time with Hunt, that is to say in 1859, I
aimed at making a realistic study of painting,
keeping to myself the designs and attempts,
serious or slight, which might have a meaning
more than that of a strict copy from nature.
I painted flowers to get the relation between
the softness and brittleness of the flower and
the hardness of the bowl or whatever it might
be in which the flower might be placed. Instead of arranging my subject, which is the
usual studio way, I had it placed for me by
chance, with any background and any light,
leaving, for instance, the choice of flowers and
vase to the servant girl or groom or any one.
Or else I copied the corner of the breakfast
table as it happened to be. You will see that
that is a reasonable method of meeting any
difficulties that come up in strict painting.

"I got quite sure that my many years' acquaintance with the works of art which were
arrangements would be sufficient to remain in
my mind while I worked in so different a way
for purposes of education. In the studio with

Hunt we (for there were three or four of us), painted from the model in his way, which was a variation of Couture's; perhaps not exactly his way but with his mixtures of paints and his kind of brush."

La Farge loved to dwell upon that period of exciting experiment and treasured all its souvenirs, especially those connected with his fellow students. Amongst these was the late William James, who drew "beautifully" he said, repeating the word three or four times. He knew Henry James also, then and thereafter. The novelist had, he said, the painter's eye, adding that few writers possessed it. In La Farge's opinion the literary man did not so much see a thing as think about it. In those old days he advised Henry James to turn writer, but, he said, he did not offer his counsel dogmatically. He simply felt vaguely that in the conflict between the two instincts in his friend the writing one seemed the stronger. He was always pleased to remember, by the way, that when Stanford White had come to him with the ambition to be a painter he had urged him, instead, to embrace architecture as his profession. Some of the gifts of the painter were there, he told me, but on the whole he felt that

White's bent for building and decoration was decisive and it interested him to observe the confirmation of his judgment in the architect's career. His friendship with William James had the special warmth springing from youthful struggles together and he delighted to talk of a meeting that they had late in life, the first in something like twenty-one years. They dined together and some time afterwards La Farge, who had spoken to me of the episode before, wrote to me about it more in detail in this letter:—

"He reminded me as we dined of our going out sketching together at the Glen, Newport, and of what I was painting then, and that I was not *copying*. On the contrary, I was merely using the facts to support my being in relation to nature. It is Rousseau who said, for painting out of doors in study, 'You can paint a chestnut well from an oak if you are in the mood to feel nature call on you.' Well, this had intrigued James all these years (fifty) and also my manner of painting. The ground of my panel was absolutely black. I should think so. It was a beautifully 'varnished' Japanese black panel[1] of which I had taken off

[1] As a matter of fact, an old tea tray, he told me.

the top shining coats to get at the dull 'preparation' underneath, on which as you know the work is based. It could not be blacker and safer. It will last a thousand years and stand being in the sea, etc. And my picture, of course, has not altered. It is in the Boston Museum. And across all those years W. J. remembered it. I explained to his satisfaction. Then he said: 'Do you remember the bread and butter, and there was a red-headed girl served us.' 'W.,' I said, 'many a red-headed girl I have met (and white horse) but I'll take this one for granted.' 'Well,' he concluded, ' John, who could have guessed then that to-day we should be sitting here, each one an authority in his own profession!' Is that James-y or not? And isn't it pretty? A few days after, at Easter, in Columbia Chapel, the clergyman preaching referred to James, not the Christian apostle, but our friend, and the views we associate with him.''

With Newport he had, for most of his life, close relations, keeping a home there and preserving the local friendships dating from his studies with Hunt, but when the latter were broken off the scenes and events of his life rapidly changed. Early in 1860 he returned to New York and for the moment abandoned painting, and in the early spring he went South to Louisiana. There the artistic faculty reasserted itself. "I drew and painted," he says, "because it was so tempting, always drawing or painting in the way of study of some special side of the things we see, and keeping secret to myself some of the drawings, which you may have seen, and which were made to illustrate Browning's poems." When he came North in May he was delayed in all his projects "and generally made doubtful of the future by having brought back from the marshes of Louisiana a bad case of malaria which for many years hung over me." He resumed his painting, starting an important picture of St. Paul preaching, for the church or chapel of his friend Father Hecker, the founder of the Paulist order, but the work went slowly. In 1860 he was married, to Miss Margaret Mason Perry. Then came the war, but, as I have previously mentioned, La Farge's eyes were not fitted for the battlefield and the effect at this time, despite poignant distractions, was simply to confirm him in the enthusiastic practice of the profession into which he had drifted. I make much

of the influences that moulded him and accordingly I speak here of his meeting with
John Bancroft, a friend who gave him still another key to the mysterious land of art. He
thus recognizes the gift : —

" The war upset all my notions of the future I had sketched out, that is to say of going
to Europe and making further studies there
and becoming definitely a painter, or at any
rate devoting myself to an artistic career.
For every reason I remained here, deeply interested in the war and regretting having no
chance to take any part in it. It was thus that
I came to know John Bancroft, who had been
down to try, but who found that he was not
fitted for anything like that, though his health
was as good as mine was bad, still broken by
the continuance of the illness acquired in the
South.

"This acquaintance with Bancroft and a
continued friendship was a serious factor in
my life. He was a student, almost too much
of one, and we plunged into the great questions of light and color which were beginning
to be laid out by the scientific men and which
later the painters were to take up. This was
the cause of a great deal of work but of less

painting, if I may say so, less picture-making, because of an almost incessant set of observations and comments and inquiries supplemented by actual work in painting. All that I have done since then has been modified by those few years of optical studies, and the last realistic painting which may have shown it is the ' Paradise Valley,' which belongs to '66–'67–'68.

"Bancroft and myself were very much interested in Japanese color prints and I imported a great many in the early sixties for us both, through A. A. Low. I think it was 1863. We had to risk our purchases entirely and got few things as we should have chosen them, as we had at that time no persons interested in such things. We had nobody over there in Japan to buy for us with any discretion. The point that interested us both has not yet, I think, been studied out. I may be wrong, but I have never heard it discussed among the people who have been influenced by Japanese printing or by the amateurs of those things. The very serious point to me was the display in certain of these color prints of landscape relations in color. This is done so simply as to give a continuous explanation of how the painter built his scheme, and for Bancroft and myself, interested in constructing similar schemes, according to modern scientific analyses, this Japanese confirmation and occasional teaching was full of most serious interest. Whether Mr. Whistler, for instance, ever saw this I do not know. Of course he and others were much interested in the beautiful arrangements of light or dark, light and color, and so on, and Mr. Whistler appreciated this and amused himself by making more of it than really was necessary to a man of his capacity.

"For a person of your intelligence and culture knows quite well that the Japanese thing in those matters is not new, that the merit of these things in the way of color, line, and space and the arrangement of the three is exactly what it has always been in the best work of every nation and every clime, as far as we know. But in the Japanese prints and in some of their paintings it is more obvious because it is less covered up. It is like a child's book in words of three syllables. It was so that any one who ran could read and at length people began to catch on. But you know this and know how foolish and childish is the talk of to-day with regard to any novelty in the principles of these now admired bits of art, which at my date endangered with amateurs the reputation of the painter who publicly admired them.

"Let us reverse this question and take an anecdote of Okakura. On one of his first days here I took him to see some wonderful Rembrandts. Okakura knelt before them and said, 'This is what the great Chinese artists in black and white meant to do.' Then he recognized carefully and analyzed the same points that we are speaking of, taking one day to study the arrangement of line and space; the next day for the study of the arrangement of black and white, and the next day again for the picture part, that told the story, the wonderful meaning and the extraordinary skill in drawing which allowed those incredible subtle meanings to be represented by a line of the etcher. As you see, he was faithful to the fundamental laws, those by which I hold, and he saw first the basis of the Rembrandt, which it has in common with all great work, and then the special beauties of Rembrandt himself."

Europe had helped La Farge and he had stretched out an acquisitive hand to the East. Literature and art, archæology and science, had all contributed to bring his genius to the point of efflorescence. Arduously, and yet with a disinterestedness that makes him seem more a type of natural and happy growth than of straining effort, he had arrived at the making of beautiful pictures.

V

HALF A CENTURY OF
PAINTING

THE title of this chapter points to the
unity in the life of a great artist which
his biographer always comes so soon to recognize. In the years of preparation external incidents stand out in sharp relief and there is
some difficulty in so coördinating them as to
show their formative influences. Then, with
the maturing of a man's gifts and their final
consecration to a single purpose, the miscellaneous events of his career, if I may so de-
fine them, fall into a more or less subordinate relation. Where he was once dominated
he now dominates. Experience may have its
initiatory significance, but on the whole it
counts more as supplying the raw material
for creative processes. The La Farge of Paul
de Saint-Victor's Paris and of wide European
wanderings, the La Farge of the Manchester
Exposition and pre-Raphaelite contacts, is a
temperament feeling its way. The La Farge
of the half-century with which I have now to
deal is simply a genius in action.

The Ascension

All that happens to him in this period is of interest more particularly as it finds expression in his work. His cup of sensation was well filled. In the early seventies he went again to Europe, which, indeed, he was not infrequently to revisit. Later he made two memorable journeys, to Japan and to the South Seas. At home he played a constructive part in the building up of an American school of art, constantly figuring in the world of exhibitions and general organization, training assistants and transmitting his knowledge not only directly to pupils but through lectures and writings. His work in glass and mural decoration had also the effect of immensely increasing the number of those episodes which diversify the purely human side of an artist's life. On more than one of those episodes we shall have occasion to pause. But it is La Farge the artist, specifically, who now engages our study, and, above all, La Farge the painter.

He first assumed that character with absolute authority in the " Paradise Valley," that Newport landscape dating from the sixties with which his recollections have already given us some little acquaintance. It is a picture of peculiar significance in the history of

American art, especially for any one of the present generation. When I first saw it, a long time ago, I found no difficulty in apprehending its beauty. There was nothing in the least esoteric about it. And yet I was a little puzzled. Impressionism, I knew, had come into American painting long after its date, and, besides, La Farge was not painting, at the moment, anything quite like it, nor had he done so for years. Yet here was a landscape, done in America while the Hudson River school was still active in the land, and preserving qualities of light and atmosphere to which that school had never even begun to attain. Also it was as emphatically modern as anything painted in the last quarter of a century. Indeed, this picture, like the masterpieces of Corot and Rousseau — to which, by the way, it owns no kinship implying the debt of the imitator — has that effect as of truth and artistic rightness which is of no date. For the critic, instinctively eager to account for so bewildering a boon, the work naturally had an extraordinary interest, and in talk with La Farge the subject was one to which we were always returning.

He himself had a lively appreciation of its

historical meaning and liked to go over the
origins of his success in landscape. It was a
hard-won success and involved, among other
things, a lavish expenditure of patience. He
built himself a little hut among the rocks,
where he would leave his picture, going back
day after day so as to get as far as possible
the same light. Fishermen broke into the hut
once, to injure the canvas, and he had trouble
with gypsies, whose prying ways threatened
disaster to his handiwork, but nothing daunted
him. He was urged on, too, by the over-
powering impulse of the discoverer, the conviction that if he could do what he had in his
mind he would push back the boundaries of
landscape art. In the " Paradise Valley," he
told me, "I undertook a combination of a large
variety of problems which were not in the line
of my fellow artists here, nor did I know of
any one in Europe who at that time undertook
them." He then elaborated the description of
his procedure : —

"My programme was to paint from nature
a portrait, and yet to make distinctly a work
of art which should remain as a type of the
sort of subject I undertook, a subject both
novel and absolutely 'everydayish.' I there-

fore had to choose a special moment of the day and a special kind of weather at a special time of the year, when I could count upon the same effect being repeated. I chose a number of difficulties in combination so as to test my acquaintance with them both in theory of color and light and in the practice of painting itself. I chose a time of day when the shadows falling away from me would not help me to model or draw, or make ready arrangements for me, as in the concoction of pictures usually; and I also took a fairly covered day, which would still increase the absence of shadows. That would be thoroughly commonplace, as we see it all the time, and yet we know it to be beautiful, like most of ' out-of-doors.' I modelled these surfaces of plain and sky upon certain theories of the opposition of horizontals and perpendiculars in respect to color and I carried this general programme into as many small points of detail as possible. I also took as a problem the question of the actual size of my painting as covering the surface which I really saw at a distance, which would be represented by the first appearance of the picture. A student of optics will understand.

"The main difficulty was to do all this from nature and to keep steadily at the same time to these theories without having them stick out, if I may say so, as some of my intelligent foreign friends managed to do. In nature nothing sticks out. My foreign friends also have since worked out similar problems but they have not always insisted upon that main one, that the problems are *not visible* in nature. Nature, meaning in this case the landscape we look at, looks as if it had done itself and had not been done by an artist."

That last remark is very characteristic of La Farge's aversion from the mere display of learning, the deliberate exaltation of personalized technique. Competent execution, as I have remarked before, he took for granted as the proper attribute of any self-respecting painter. There is a delightful instance of this in a letter of his to Miss Barnes, embodying much the same analysis of the same picture as that given in the foregoing quotation. "This, of course," he concludes, "has nothing to do with the actual technique employed in the painting, about which any artist of knowledge can judge." It was just about that time, in 1869, that he was made a member of the

Academy of Design. However he may have
struck his new colleagues we may be certain
of one thing, that he gave them furiously to
think. I can cite no contemporary criticism of
the "Paradise Valley" in particular, but there
is one available passage on his work in that
period from the pen of a coeval and friend. It
occurs in "The Digressions of V," the charming autobiography in which Elihu Vedder has
only lately told us of his early impressions of
art and artists. Speaking of his experiences
in Boston just after the war he says: —

"I always connect La Farge with the Boston of that time. If Hunt was comforting, La
Farge was inspiring; I have never met any
one more so, and it was only my impervious-
ness that prevented my profiting more by his
advice and example. It was at this time he
painted those flowers — one might say truthfully his flowers; I had never seen anything
like them then, and I have never seen anything like them since. At this time I remember Doll having for sale that wonderful little
picture of La Farge's, — the old Newport
house with its large roof covered with snow,
standing solemnly in the gloom of an over-
cast winter day, — not only wonderful in

sentiment, but for the truth of the transmitted
light through the snow-burdened air. I went
to Doll's one day with the firm intention of
becoming the happy possessor of this little
picture, but La Farge by some subtle instinct
must have scented danger, and I found it was
no longer for sale. This quality of subtlety is
shown in those never-to-be-forgotten flowers,
particularly in that damp mass of violets in a
shallow dish on a window-sill, where the outside air faintly stirring the lace curtains seems
to waft the odour towards you. This quality,
peculiarly his own, affects me in his writings,
so that as a writer I was at one time inclined
to find fault with him for a certain elaborate
obscurity in his style, which I now see arises
from his striving to express shades of thought
so delicate that they seem to render words almost useless. Therefore his words seem to
hover about a thought as butterflies hover
about the perfume of a flower."

In this evocation of the very life of nature
La Farge was unapproachable among painters
of flowers, save by the French Fantin-Latour
and the American Maria Oakey Dewing, one
of his own pupils. To say of a master in this
field that he interprets the soul of a flower is

to risk a certain misunderstanding, for the
phrase may so readily be made to point to
imaginative and even "literary" ideas of
which the painter never dreamed. Yet there
is no other phrase so delicately, so truthfully
descriptive. Anatole France, to whom I find
myself so often returning as I think of La
Farge, recalls George Sand's reverie over
some wild sage that had left its perfume on
her hands, and, many miles away, had stirred
her to affectionate remembrance. She waxed
poetic on the theme. We have all shared in
her experience. We are all, in other words,
aware of something more than sensuous
beauty in a flower, something that seems
really among the things of the spirit. So La
Farge painted his flowers, with an indescribable tenderness. His vision pierced deeper than
that of the artist who would deal in forthright,
domineering fashion with "things seen." He
could not shake off the glamour of things
unseen but felt. Like that veil on which Flaubert is so magnificent there was always a
beauty just beyond his reach. And yet, as I
cannot too often emphasize, there went hand in
hand with his subtle, spiritualized conception
of art, that habit of the scientific inquirer and

the experimentalist in technique which allied him to the great realists in painting. Here is his reply to inquiries of mine about his early flower paintings, some of them going as far back as 1859 : —

"My painting of flowers was in great part a study; that is, a means of teaching myself many of the difficulties of painting, some of which are contradictory, as, for example, the necessity of extreme rapidity of workmanship and very high finish. Many times in painting flowers I painted right on without stopping, painting sometimes far into the night or towards morning while the flower still retained the same shade, which it was sure to lose soon. This obliged me also to know the use of my colors and the principles of the use of the same, for the difference between daylight and lamplight is very great, and the colors as one sees them in one light are not the colors of another. That we all know, as even the ladies do who wear different colors for night from what they do for the day.

"Thinking again about the pictures of flowers which I used to paint, there were, besides the paintings that were studies of the flowers, and those that were painted as pic-

tures, certain ones in which I tried to give
something more than a study or a handsome
arrangement. Some few were paintings of the
water lily, which has, as you know, always
appealed to the sense of something of a meaning — a mysterious appeal such as comes to us
from certain arrangements of notes of music.
Hence, I was not surprised a few weeks ago
to find a design for a frame of one of these
paintings of the water lily, treated as 'the'
water lily, not 'a' water lily. The frame had
a few bars of one of Schumann's songs, which
was written to Heine's verses, —

"Du, schöne weisse Blume,
Kanst du das Lied verstehn?

"I cannot tell, of course, whether in these
two or three attempts I have done something
more than a mere handsome representation,
but the intention I had, and consequently I
painted with great care, so carefully that the
paintings probably looked easily done because
of their real finish, which did not show any of
what Mr. Whistler calls finish."

It is in the period from which most of these
flower paintings are derived that we come
upon one of the delightful interludes in La

Farge's artistic development, like his excursions into the crafts and into sculpture, which denote his inexhaustible energy and the passion of the artist to be forever fashioning something with his hands. When Ticknor and Fields started "The Riverside Magazine," a periodical for the young, and the editor, the late Horace Scudder, was looking for good illustrations, the only artist who gave him solid satisfaction, he wrote to William Rossetti, was La Farge. The latter, hampered by ill-health, nevertheless continued to draw. For an edition of "Enoch Arden," published by the same firm, he did some of his work "bolstered up in bed," the blocks going to press a few minutes after the engraver had pulled his proof. In the "Rossetti Papers," where Scudder's letter is printed, the English poet's brother gives also this extract from his diary for April, 1868:—

"Showed Gabriel the photographs sent me by Scudder after designs ('Piper of Hamelin,' etc.) by La Farge; he was much pleased with them, and took them off to show to Brown."

They pleased La Farge. I think he kept a soft spot in his heart for these waifs and strays of his young manhood, and one evidence of this is the manner in which, long afterwards, he would occasionally make further use of their motives. The design of a seated actor made for Browning's "Men and Women" ultimately reappeared in the memorial window to Edwin Booth, and when he was painting his "Socrates," for the Supreme Court at St. Paul, he told me that he was amusing himself by reproducing in the charioteer and his horses one of his early drawings. At the time when these were made his plans were generous in scope. For Browning's poems he contemplated producing over three hundred drawings, and he started upon an edition of the Gospels for Mr. Houghton. He and Scudder were in very warm sympathy, greatly fostered by the admiration they shared for the chaotic genius of William Blake; and the two, artist and editor, projected a wonderful series of a hundred or more illustrations for the "Riverside." La Farge's idea was to develop fantasies, "imaginary representations or fairly accurate representations of historic incidents which were doubtful or of such a poetic nature as to pass easily into fairyland." He thought, too, of taking subjects from Greek history and Egyptian tradition, far-away themes, the more

remote the better, and his imagination rested
fondly on the idea of witches. Comparatively
few of these illustrations were actually en-
graved, and printed at the time — two or
three in the "Songs from Old Dramatists"
and a handful in Scudder's magazine — but
these few are of deep interest. Academic critics were then a little disposed to question the
thoroughness of La Farge's handling of the
figure, and perhaps they were right; but if he
was somewhat deficient in matters of anatom-
ical structure there was nothing in his workmanship to diminish the force of his inventive
faculty. His "Bishop Hatto," his "Giant," his
"Fisherman and the Afrite" are wonderfully
poetic creations, enveloped in the true spirit
of romance. In one particular instance he
bodied forth a fantastic idea with extraordinary power. "The Wolf Charmer" gives a
haunting reality to a figure that never existed.
How deeply it interested him may be judged
by the fact that he took up the subject again,
afterwards, in other mediums, ultimately producing the large version in oils now in the public museum at St. Louis.

This painting is an impressive manifestation
of La Farge's genius for the illustration of po-

etic feeling. The central idea is not precisely either historical or dramatic. This page out of the folk lore of Brittany tells no very elaborate story. The piper who draws the wolves after him with his piping may be the hero of any number of eerie narratives recited by rustic firesides, but the tales told about him have not crystallized in a single fabric of romance universally known. His charm is vague and subtle. It consists, when all is said, in just the incongruity of a human being consorting with wild beasts on some strange understanding that might in an instant be broken, with disastrous results. It is music that is the tenuous bond between this uncouth shepherd and his green-eyed, slavering flock. Were the notes to cease but for a moment the man who seems to be the master would be torn by the brutes that follow his wild strain. That, at all events, is one of the thoughts provoked by this picture; the imagination is filled with a sense of crouching terrors, of forest mysteries, of adventure in a world that to the mortal eye is a sealed book. La Farge, with the magic of his art, makes us free of that world.

It is characteristic of him that he does this not with the aid of grotesque accessories or

with the ingenious manipulation of light and
shade, but by the simple process of giving
the piper and his wolves intense reality. The
weird, huddled procession comes toward us
through a passage between giant rocks, and
beyond these we see the forest, a place of
vast tree trunks and illimitable distances. The
murmuring silence of the wildwood is there,
and in it we feel that anything is possible, even
this monstrous companionship of man and
beast. There is a great deal contributing to
the effect of the picture in the details of movement and gesture. The piper bent over his
task and slowly advancing, the wolves pad-
ding around and after him, bring many unob-
trusive but weighty touches of expression into
the scheme. But it is as a unit of imaginative
design that "The Wolf Charmer" bewilders
and enchants. It produces an illusion as of
something seen in a dream, poignantly realized while the dream lasts, and yet apprehended, as things are so often apprehended in
a dream, with an indefinable consciousness of
supernatural implications. It is as though the
living world and the world of faery were made
one in a kind of vision.

When the painting was exhibited it met

with some criticism, again with reference to
details of structure in the forms, and La Farge
had some things to tell me on that point. He
said that people might argue that the animals
were not truthfully drawn, but there was a
reason for the lines he had adopted. He was
not trying to represent nature but to create
the atmosphere of the little German poem
that had first put the idea of "The Wolf
Charmer" into his head. In that poem, he
said, the wolf was an eerie idea, chiefly, not
literally a beast of fur and fangs. So when he
made the original drawing, years ago, the one
for the wood-cut, he made many studies of
jackals and hyenas and deliberately mingled
their traits with those of the true wolf in his
design. He told me, by the way, that his old
professor in anatomy, Dr. Rimmer, deprecated his making so many studies, with the
remark, "When you make so many studies
you discharge your memory." La Farge ad-
mitted that there was a good deal in this but
somehow the study idea had always appealed
to his sense of artistic duty and he had filled
countless sketch books in the course of his life.
About "The Wolf Charmer" he told me an
incident that had given him immense plea-

sure. When he went to Japan he met there a
court painter, now dead, one Hung Ai. "Oh,
you are the wolf man," exclaimed this artist,
instantly remembering him as the maker of
the design which he knew in the old engraving. He also surprised La Farge by
guessing that some of the work had been done
with a Japanese brush — he said he recognized the "stroke" — which happened to be
the fact. Besides the original drawing and the
large painting La Farge did, somewhere between the two, a water color of "The Wolf
Charmer" for the late William C. Whitney,
for whom he had also at first intended the
version in oils. Whitney, it seems, wanted to
be his backer. La Farge told him that it made
him think of the elephant who adopted the
family of a heartless hen, and to take care of
the chickens sat on them. Still, the alliance between patron and painter might have been
effected, but just then Whitney died.

The anecdote carries us far from the period
of the flower paintings and the Newport landscapes, but in any case it would be necessary
to note here, not a divergence from the central principles on which they were based but
indubitably a modification of La Farge's man-

ner. In the leisurely experiments of the fifties
and the following decade he had achieved exquisite beauty of surface. If he had gone on
exactly as he had begun, and, moreover, had
narrowly pursued that special quality, we
know just where he would have ranged himself. Save for the poetic and religious motives which were bound to pass into his work
he would have become the Alfred Stevens of
this country, winning fame through nothing
more nor less than the consummate kneading
of pigment. But, as I trust I have sufficiently
indicated, La Farge, while appreciating the
value of such fame to the full, was so consti-
tuted intellectually and in all the subtleties of
his being that he could not with any satisfaction have sought it for himself. His imagination took a vastly wider sweep. There were
too many other fields to conquer. Furthermore, this time of transition was to witness his
first excursion into mural decoration and the
growth of his interest in glass. There is, therefore, something like a movement of disloca-
tion, gradual, scarcely perceptible, but unmistakable none the less, of which one is conscious
on taking leave of the early paintings. Different employments have their quiet influence

upon the pictures that succeed them, an influence telling simply and solely in this matter of
surface. It is still beautiful, but, for the gour-
met in such things, less beguiling for its own
sake. The magic of pure painting which flour-
ishes in the sixties but yields in the seventies
to the broader and necessarily less lacquer-like
texture imposed by the exigencies of wall
painting, gives place, finally, to the manner
illustrated by the Japanese and South Sea
souvenirs.

It is not a question of values but of differences, and, indeed, the later work, if it
lacks the curious *bloom* of the first paintings,
has other rich sources of charm and is even,
in one respect, much more powerful. La
Farge's two famous journeys to the South
and East gave him a firmer grasp upon light
and air and tremendously enriched his color.
His early tones have an incomparable softness and delicacy, but I remember a flower
piece of his, a study of the flaming Hibiscus
found in the Society Islands, which gave one
a new and almost startling sense of what he
could do when he had tasted the hot inspiration
of the tropics. The red petals fairly blazed,
but — and the point interestingly recalled one

to the continuity of La Farge's practice — the
piercing key of his motive was kept splendidly
in hand, being modulated down through depths
of rich green foliage into peaceful shadows.
The old instinct for perfect balance remained,
but how, under such overwhelming skies,
could even La Farge have stopped to recapture the fragile tenderness of his early studies,
supposing for a moment that he might have
thought it worth while? Light, magnificent
light, intoxicated him and drove him to a
swifter and bolder notation of the things he
saw. His first impression on his arrival in Japan in the summer of 1886 is of the "splen-
dour of light," of which he never tires. "It is
as if the sky, in its variations, were the great
subject of the drama we are looking at, or at
least its great chorus. The beauty of the light
and of the air is what I should like to describe,
but it is almost like trying to account for one's
own mood — like describing the key in which
one plays." Whether he is working in oils or
in water colors — and he used both mediums
on his travels — he seizes with the same skill,
the same feeling for its diaphanous quality, the
glory of light. His color, thus bathed and
interpenetrated, grows purer, subtler, some-

times more clangorous and always more beautiful. We miss the old bloom but we do not regret it.

For one thing, La Farge never more authoritatively put technique in its place as a means to an end than in his Oriental and Pacific studies. When he made those journeys we may be sure that it was not merely to feed the lust of the eye but to come to close quarters with all the ways of foreign and notably mysterious peoples, barbaric in the Fiji Islands or thereabouts, and in the East possessing a civilization equally different from anything to which he was accustomed. For many a "travel note" in modern art a photograph might easily be substituted. La Farge on his travels made his lightest sketch a thing of enchanting originality. As through some curious wave of inner illumination you are made aware among his pictures not simply of mountain and valley, of sea and sky, but of the very genius of a far scene. When he painted "The Hereditary Assassins of King Malietoa" he made manifest all that was uncanny about those personages. When, in Japan, he portrayed "The Priest of Idzumo Watching at Dawn for the Soul of the Dragon Which Comes in With the May

Tides," you shared the strange vigil of the bizarre figure on the seashore. And, while La Farge's affair with his picturesque models, who were going so naturally about one business or other incredible to any Western mind save a mind like his, was thus profoundly an affair of interpretation, he never forgot that the mere facts observed were but substances and alloys to be thrown into the furnace of his art and there fused into a unit of design. I turn to one more of his South Sea impressions, typical of his constructive habit. It is a picture of a ford on the Tautira River, the record of an incident of no particular importance. Three women are crossing the ford. One of them stands in the shallows on the farther side, a dimly outlined figure. The second is just striking out, and shows only her head and shoulders above the water. The third comes running down the bank, apparently to take the plunge a moment later. The action represented is artlessness itself. But La Farge gets an indescribable and very beautiful sequence of movement out of his three figures. He paints their graceful forms against a luxuriant background, above which rise purple peaks, and he draws all of the wild beauty of the scene into a pictorial harmony so simple, and, withal, having such an air of finality about it, that the thing seems invented until you realize its superb truth. In his analysis of Delacroix in "The Higher Life in Art" he has a passage which is apposite to our present subject. Speaking of the great problem of movement in art he says : —

"As with Rodin, who is a great example, as with Barye, Delacroix's friend, as with the Greeks, as with the greater men of all time, except the present, so Delacroix felt the unexpressed rule that the human being never moves free in *space*, but always, being an animal, in relation to the place where he is, to the people around him, to innumerable influences of light, and air, wind, footing, and the possibility of touching others. This is the absolute contradiction of the studio painting, however dignified, where the figure is free from any interruption, and nobody will run against it."

The principle was as the breath of life to his own work. His use of it accounts for the amazing vitality and naturalness of his numerous studies of South Sea dancers and it is implicit also in his pictures of figures nominally immobile. One such is a certain painting of

chiefs in war dress, another Fijian note. The
seated soldiers in this composition are, if you
like, doing nothing at all. They are merely
posed in a double row — if, again, you so
choose to consider them — in order that the
artist might make his sketch. But he makes
more than a sketch. His sitters are types and
in their lovely landscape the suggestion they
convey is as of a page from Fijian life. There
is something dark and sinister about the
group. There is nothing of the company of
docile models, posing as so many types of
form and color. There is everything of a
curious state of savagery, of men in whose
traits and demeanor you recognize the marks
of a peculiar social state. So it is with all of
La Farge's exotic studies, exotic for us but
not for him, for it always has seemed to me
that he was completely and restfully at home
in the lands of the lotus-eater, amongst long-
robed, suave Japanese priests or amongst the
stalwart chiefs and laughing maidens of the
Pacific. It is with a wrench that we retrace
our steps to follow him upon the busy path
of the mural painter, collaborating with architects, facing conditions of the most practical nature, and adapting his wayward, ad-

Moses receiving the Law on Mount Sinai

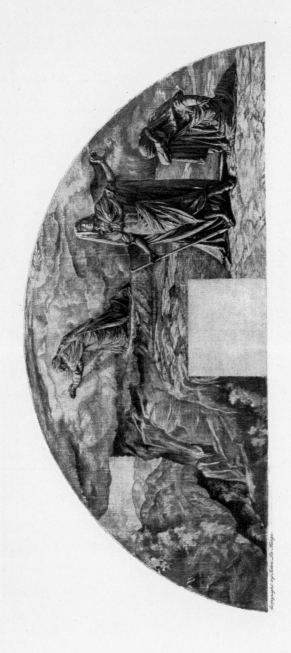

venturous genius to the discipline of perhaps the most exacting of all the arts of design.

As usual with him the new opportunity
was not deliberately sought but arose in slow,
inevitable fashion out of his personal associations and out of the intellectual processes
which were always extending his horizon. I
lay stress upon the point, for one of the most interesting and revealing things about La Farge
is his freedom from anything like malice
aforethought, from preconceived resolution,
in his different undertakings. He was a man
of inspiration, not necessarily sudden leaps
into new spheres, but ventures implying the
guidance of that "familiar" so often en-
countered in the history of genius. He goes
whole-heartedly along through one channel
of endeavor and then, when the appointed
time comes, he invades another. I say "invades," for at these moments you feel that he
has had all along just the right preparation
and is somehow equipped for whatever re-
sponsibilities may befall. His assumption of
those of the mural decorator dates from the
seventies, not many years after his second
journey abroad, but in origin it is traceable to

an earlier date, to old studies and to old friendships. It is to the latter especially that he refers in the recollections that bear upon his
work in Trinity Church at Boston, the scene
of his first dealings with large wall spaces.
They go back to the formation of his intimacy
with the architect of that building: —

" I had known H. H. Richardson for some
few years, meeting him first in George Post's
office. George introduced him as a clever man
who would make his mark. He was then designing something of his own, a Gothic church
based upon a rather strict view of Gothic principles. He knew almost nothing of Gothic,
being fresh from 'Beaux Arts' of the worst
possible kind, but the thing was striking and
as I came out I said to Post, 'That looks
something like the beginning of genius.' Just
before his death, years afterwards, Richardson
reproached me for my admiration of his drawing, which had rankled, apparently, all those
years. As we know, he became a type of Romanesque and he told me that the thing had
been 'damned bad,' and how could I have admired it? I told him with my usual frankness
that I thought so too; but what I had told Post
was that he was probably a genius, which has

nothing to do with accuracy of design in a style of which one is ignorant.

"We saw a good deal of each other, as any men might who had a former Parisian habit. The American architects had not yet begun experience of the École des Beaux Arts, but Richardson had had it in full, and had earned his living in the offices of French architects, so that he knew the whole machine. He told me once, in contempt for the past, that if he had enough offices he could build from New York to New Orleans without giving himself any trouble except to order the designs. And he had been a militant, joining the young men who hissed away Viollet-le-Duc from his lectures, from a mixture of anti-Gothic and anti-Napoleon the Third opinions. But the meaning of all these things did not trouble his mind once the sea was crossed. Then he took up the grind here, which was severe, and soon was fairly successful. I forget how the first work went on. Then began his tendency towards the Romanesque, but nothing serious, so that when he competed in the most courageous way, with Dick Hunt, among others, for Trinity Church, and won, he had, as yet, not taken hold seriously of the Romanesque problem. He designed a building which was intelligent but not what could be done and especially wanting in any historical character. Gradually he felt it. We spent many hours together. He was then at Staten Island, a married man, and glad to give me long day and night hospitality. Like many other great men he was a mighty eater and drinker — a pitcher of milk, a pitcher of champagne, a pitcher of water — everything was done on a large scale and his work is of that kind. He used to speak of *'l'échelle,'* which he did not understand, unless perhaps in the last few months of his life, when he had been in Spain. I was able to propose to Richardson to change entirely the character of his building, so far at least as externals, which in this case would not be separated from the great basis of plan, etc. I brought him photographs of the Spanish Romanesque churches, Avila, and so forth, of which I had a special collection, made for Queen Victoria during her visit. Meanwhile, Richardson built the Brattle Street church.''

Regarding this church La Farge had a picturesque association, relating to the relief high up on the tower which was carried out by Bartholdi. The French sculptor had come to this country just after *l'année terrible,* to work on his statue of Liberty Enlightening the World. This had been planned before the Franco-Prussian war by a committee anxious to make some political demonstration of French Republicans to the United States, which country they felt to be in some dangerous relation to the plans of Napoleon III. He produced the model for the present statue in La Farge's studio and there he made the acquaintance of Richardson. "They were soon friends," writes La Farge, "which makes all the prettier a little speech of Richardson's to Bartholdi when Bartholdi, naturally interested in Richardson's long stay in France, inquired if he did not like the French, and Richardson replied, 'No, not at all.' One of the best known sculptors in the country had been asked to carry out the relief for the Brattle Street church, and he had declined it, because in his opinion it might level him to the position of a stone-cutter and for the public it would not look well. Hence Bartholdi was asked and was only too glad to have the fun of preparing the models in France, to be carried out here later. In the relief as it was put up were several por-

traits, including those of Richardson and myself." But we must return to Trinity Church.

In the early seventies La Farge's hold upon
landscape had not seemed to be slackening.
The "Paradise Valley" had won him honor.
But even then, he said, he had "become
tempted and then drawn to work in the lines
of architecture," and presently the decisive
step was taken: —

"It was thus that I came to decorate Trinity
Church, Boston, which was being built by my
friend Richardson, who believed in me without
having much proof of what I could do in that
way. The early part of September, 1876, was
the time at which the architect gave me first
notice of the work to be done and the first of
January was to be the final end. That was to
include the entire building, from the first talk to
the finished work. The building, as you know,
was not finished then, there being no roof on
part of it, nor windows, nor possible scaffold-
ing, nor designs that were accurate. There
were also no people. I managed to get an extension of several weeks so that February saw
the work through. The designs that were to
be painted in the day had often to be made on
the previous night. We had to enlist any one.

. . . The amusing point to me was the application of certain Romanesque originals to the spans I had before me and the introduction of a great deal of very fine and calculated detail into passages of necessary simplicity, and also the doing of this at a gallop. I think that in one space, fifteen feet square, there is not more than three or four days' work, and everything was done in that way, but with extreme care, a care I have very rarely seen repeated in any modern work by anybody, unless perhaps we take some of the work of Mr. Sargent, on which he has spent years and years of careful thought and elaboration. Part of my work, you know, is hidden by the facing of the organ at the west end, so that that elaboration is hidden and the lines of my general composition are more or less destroyed. So of course all through the building the new additions are not connected with the old lines.

"I must tell you about the jamboree in which we carried out the work — the windows open, in winter; four of the workmen killed by the tiles dropping down from the roof inside; we working with our overcoats and gloves, unable to use the scaffoldings very often because the other workmen, masons, carpenters, tilers, etc. who were not painters, had them. And even Phillips Brooks, thank God, as I told him, came near being killed by a plank which had dropped down from one hundred feet above his head. I thanked the Lord because then the committee put in an extra man, to watch the hole through which the planks and tiles dropped on poor devils and future bishops."

The absolute novelty of the undertaking had, of course, much to do with these untoward conditions. American mural decoration was then in the process of being born, the only contemporary of La Farge's making any serious contribution to it being his old friend William Hunt, who, at just about that time, was to do his interesting work in the Capitol at Albany. There were clever artists to be got hold of as assistants, after all, but they had to be trained. That they were trained by him and were in the fullest sense assistants, subject to his control, was a matter on which La Farge liked a clear understanding. He was generosity itself in appreciation of what these men did to enable him to execute his commission in so ridiculously short a time; he remembered their services, as he valued their abilities. But I remember his indignation when on the death of Francis Lathrop there got into print a "crazy statement," as he described it to me, which assigned to that admirable artist a far more constructive share in the work at Trinity than had actually been his. La Farge straightway sent a correction to the journal in error, and, writing to me about it to ask that I would establish the record, he said, "It is a bore, but I wish the fact known that I had the charge of ten to fifteen artists, Frank Millet, George Maynard, John Du Fais, Francis Lathrop, Sidney L. Smith, George L. Rose, etc. who did exactly what I wanted as far as they knew how."

The astonishing thing is that in spite of the novelty of his task, the physical handicaps —including ill-health—and the demon of hurry at his elbow, La Farge nevertheless gave fair unity to his large scheme. Strictly speaking, however, that was not, at that moment, the all-important point. It would no doubt have been better if he could have had more time and had established then a thoroughly organic conception of mural painting. But it was a momentous achievement simply to have demonstrated the power and beauty

of the mere idea of wall painting. La Farge
could do this because he could communicate
to his designs the compelling quality of style,
and, besides, the vitalizing force of mind and
imagination. There are merits of sheer color
in the Trinity paintings, as there are merits
of the shrewd adjustment of painted detail to
the architectural whole; but most significant
of all in their historical aspect are the grand
hieratic figures set upon the walls, solemn
presences, which loom like living prophets in
the richly Romanesque interior, and the beautiful angels, who have an even more formally
decorative purpose but possess also a graceful, light charm. La Farge might fall short
of perfection in this very ambitious attempt,
thanks to no fault of his own, but it was
immediately apparent that if any American
painter could reach that goal in mural decoration he was the man.

From that time onward to the day of his
death he was the recognized leader in work
of this character, and important commissions
rapidly succeeded one another. I have no intention of traversing them all, — the beautiful panels in the Church of the Incarnation
in New York, those others for St. Thomas's

Church in the same city which were not long ago destroyed by fire, the exquisite decorations, " Music " and " Drama," in the music room of the New York house of the Hon. Whitelaw Reid, and many other noble productions. The list is far too long. Furthermore, all of this work was quietly carrying him on to an impressive culmination, the crystallization of his decorative genius in the monumental forms characteristic of the great masters in all ages. La Farge's lyrical vein was ineradicable. When he came to paint the Reid decorations, in the eighties, his early sensitiveness to landscape was revived in full force and he placed amid sylvan surroundings figures of a poetic sentiment and grace which would suggest Watteau, if it were not that they bear the stamp of La Farge's fuller, statelier, and more realistic sense of form. But in that very period he was working out one of his profoundest problems, that of "The Ascension" for the church of that name in New York. In one of his letters he tells me how he arrived at the solution which we know : —

"In the picture of 'The Ascension' in the Tenth Street church there were some very

curious problems. The clergyman had liked
a drawing which I had made many years before, let us say some thirty years ago, of that
subject, with a similar grouping. This was to
be a very narrow high window for a memorial chapel out West. It was never carried
out; in fact it was nothing but one of those
projects forced upon unfortunate artists by
enthusiastic millionaires who forget almost
immediately what their last plans had been.
I do not even know if anything was done
about it, but the proposed patron was interesting, owing to his having very many works
of art, some of which were fine and the others
not usually seen in this country even to-day
— not that they were good.

"Then Dr. Donald, the clergyman, hap-
pening to see this, wished to have this long
and narrow window carried out where you
now see the painting; there being a recess in
the wall, it might be used. At that time I was
very anxious to have Saint-Gaudens get a
chance to do work and to show his capacity.
Remember that I am talking of very many
years ago. I proposed that he might, perhaps,
be tempted to make a great bas-relief of this
to fill that space; but there were too many

reasons against it, among others those of money. A painting can be done, it is supposed, quite cheaply compared to a piece of sculpture, even if that sculpture is only in plaster at a few cents a foot.

"By and by, when Stanford White took charge of the church, the questions came together and it was proposed that I should paint the picture upon the wide space which he left for it. But that space was many, many times wider than the sketch or study and even enlarging the figures in enormous proportions would not fill it. Even now the picture is almost square, so that I had a problem of widening my space of figures and of settling their proportion in a given space. Nothing that I could do, and keep the original intention, would allow the change to be done to cover enough space, so that I proposed a frame which should both cut a little space, indicate the Gothic character of the church, and help what I thought I was going to do to carry out the painting — that was to place these figures in a very big landscape. The landscape I wished to have extremely natural, because I depended on it to make my figures also look natural and to account for the floating of some

twenty figures or more in the air. We do not
see this ever, as you know, but I knew that
by a combination of the clouds and figures I
might help this look of what the mystic people call levitation.

"Of course you may well suppose that I
studied what I could of the people who are
swung in ropes and other arrangements across
theatres and circuses. The question of the
composition of the figures had to meet certain
geometric conditions in my mind; that is to
say, to fit a given pattern which I thought fortunate in the space. I forget whether it was an
arrangement of hexagons but I have a faint
belief that it was, owing to the arithmetical
figures of the proportions of the space. That
could be settled, but my landscape, — I was
much troubled.

"At that moment I was asked to go to Japan by my friend Henry Adams, and I went
there in 1886. I had a vague belief that I
might find there certain conditions of line
in the mountains which might help me. Of
course the Judean mountains were entirely out
of question, all the more that they implied a
given place. I kept all this in mind and on one
given day I saw before me a space of moun-

tain and cloud and flat land which seemed to me to be what was needed. I gave up my other work and made thereupon a rapid but very careful study, so complete that the big picture is only a part of the amount of work put into the study of that afternoon. There are turns of the tide which allow you at times to do an amount of work incredible in sober moments; as you know, there are very many such cases; I do not understand it myself. When I returned I was still of the same mind. My studies of separate figures were almost ready and all I had to do was to stretch the canvas and begin the work.

"Perhaps you do not know that I got into great difficulties thereupon. The weight of such a canvas is something very great. The mere lead paint used to fasten it was far over five hundred pounds. The wall, that is to say, the plaster wall, was a new one, just made, and I felt dubious about its standing this weight, when, as you know, the canvas is fastened down and then pulled flat by a great many men. It was just as I surmised. The wall tumbled down as soon as the canvas was put up, or, rather, when the first part of it was fastened. They were careful about the next wall and I believe that it is now a safe one.

"After that I only had pleasure out of my work. During that summer my friend Oka-kura spent a great deal of his time with me and I could paint, and then, in the intervals, we could talk about spiritual manifestations and all that beautiful wonderland which they have; that is to say, the Buddhists, where the spiritual bodies take form and disappear again and the edges of the real and the imaginary melt. I had one objection brought up by a friend, a lady, who was troubled by certain news she had heard. That was that I had made these studies of clouds in a pagan country, while a true Episcopalian would make them, I suppose, in England. Otherwise I think people have liked this and everybody has been very kind about it. At a distance the picture is not injured, I think, by the rapidity of its execution, only a summer and an autumn, during which I carried out several other large things."

If a painter could put into words what he puts upon canvas he would perhaps turn writing man instead. La Farge naturally passes from the little facts connected with the genesis of his work to just the pleasure that he got

out of it. We hear nothing of the intricate de-
velopments which left upon his painting the
stamp of a great creative affirmation. In that
you read not only his insight into a sublime
subject but his grasp upon a problem which
was both decorative and architectural. The
painting over the chancel in the Church of
the Ascension fills half the height of the fairly
lofty edifice. Its width is virtually the width of
the nave. These dimensions it would be idle
to state in feet and inches, but they are important to remember broadly, because the design
is so well scaled to its surroundings and seems
to spring naturally from that end of the church
over which it presides. The architectural lines
which meet the surface of the painting mark
neither a frame nor an aperture in the wall.
The richly coffered arch of gold, springing
from pilasters as generously embellished with
conventional ornament, seems rather like some
natural boundary, narrowing the horizon and
concentrating the vision upon one moving
scene. Yet, if the eyes travel, you are aware
of no conflict between the scene and its en-
circling architecture; if the transition from
one to the other is unconsciously achieved, you
must seek the secret of the passage in the

painting and not in the arch. Then you begin to grasp the beauty of a perfect wall painting. You see the harmony between the upright figures in the first plane of the composition and the pilasters on each side. And then, as you are insensibly lifted by the spring of the golden arch, the angels who encircle the risen Christ seem to float in similarly soaring line. The central figure, as it half pauses in its ascension, is the pivot of the imaginative conception, the pivot of the arrangements of forms in the group of celestial worshippers, and, finally, the pivot of the architectural lines.

Take an even more subtle point in the disposition of the lines and contours in this painting. As the spectator faces the altar he is dimly sensible of the forward leap of that arch which is reared above the aisle on each side of the church and nearest the chancel. The line is in contradiction to that of the arch above the painting. One comes towards you, the other is calculated to melt into the distance which is suggested by the receding angle of the golden arch's soffit. Now this contradiction, if left unbalanced, might prove seriously detrimental to the unity of the picture, so we

find in the latter a landscape the hills of which
are so inclined on each side as to bring the
curves of the entire scheme back into repose
and symmetry. It is not easy to demonstrate
this with mathematical precision but to look
closely at the painting, trying to imagine the
hills at the sides either eliminated or inclined
toward the mountain in the middle of the
background, is decisively to feel the force of
the point at issue. The unity of the thing
would instantly be endangered. I lay such
stress upon this side of the design, not to re-
duce its charm to a bald question of line and
mass, but to show how much its beauty depends upon the adjustment of its parts to sur-
rounding conditions. It is the felicity of this
adjustment that leaves you free to approach
the work on its imaginative and personal side,
on the side of its color and purely sensuous
enchantment. Yet even here the atmosphere
of organic balance is still enveloping the picture. The subdued light by which its lower
portion is suffused is suited not only to the
demands of the composition, but to the structure and lighting of the church at that level;
and the misty golden radiance of the upper
half is keyed to the very note that golden

arch and clerestory windows join in producing.

Thus far I have traced the beauty of La Farge's decoration to its coöperation with the architectural ideas expressed in the same place. But it is the painter's own ideas that crown his work, those, and the force with which he makes the picture a symbol for a spiritual idea. In the first place he is strikingly original. The rough outline of the composition was settled centuries ago for hundreds of masters and they were settled for him in the same way; yet through the subtleties of grouping and gesture he has escaped the faintest suggestion of any of his predecessors. If he recalls them at all it is in the sincerity with which he has bodied forth his idea. The Christ rises with thrilling dignity above the astonished worshippers who gaze in awe upon His flight, and the benignant gesture, familiar as it is, has yet in this modern painting a vitality for which hitherto we have had to go to the old Italians. Indeed, there is nothing more interesting about this design than its proof of the strength still living in sacred art when the painter is a man of genius as well as a finished craftsman. In all that makes religious art re-

ligious this is a just equivalent for the art of
an older faith. In the presence of the sacred
pictures of the fourteenth and fifteenth centuries we talk of an illusion which we fear
has since been lost, and declare that the day
for Biblical illustration is gone by. La Farge
gives the best possible answer to this pessi-
mistic conclusion. Nobly designed, flooded
with color of the deepest splendor and most
exquisite delicacy, imbued with the spirituality
of a high imagination, his painting puts before
you, on the heroic scale which it demands, the
scene which marks the culmination of our
Christian faith. It must be a cold temperament which could find in this uplifting creation less of fervor, less of the power to con-
vince, than we are willing to believe a more
naive epoch found in its more naive productions.

La Farge never painted anything more
purely beautiful than " The Ascension " and
it might not unreasonably be taken as sum-
ming up his qualities as a mural decorator;
but there is one other triumph of his in this
field upon which I wish to dwell, partly on
account of its magnitude and even more in
view of its intellectual and architectonic vir-

tues. When Mr. Cass Gilbert designed the
monumental State Capitol of Minnesota at
St. Paul, some eight or nine years ago, he was
permitted by the authorities to carry out his
idea of completing the building in a spirit
worthy of a great commonwealth. To this
end he arranged for a number of mural decorations on a large scale from various hands.
To La Farge was assigned a weighty share
in the task. For the Supreme Court room he
was commissioned to execute four paintings,
filling spacious lunettes. In the first of these
he dealt with "The Moral and Divine Law,"
his central figure being Moses kneeling on
Mount Sinai. In the second lunette he concerned himself with "The Relation of the
Individual to the State," representing a discussion between Socrates and his friends. The
next painting in the series treats of "The Recording of Precedents" and Confucius dominates here, busied with his pupils over the
collation and transcription of documents. Finally, in commemoration of "The Adjustment of Conflicting Interests," the artist
shows Count Raymond of Toulouse swearing
at the altar, in the presence of ecclesiastical
and civic dignitaries, to observe the liberties

of the city. "In each one of these four paintings," says La Farge, in a brief statement
printed at the time, "the intention has been to
give to each separate work the sense of a
special and different historical moment. Consequently of a very different attitude of mind
in the actors of each drama. For this purpose,
also, differing lights and colors for each picture." Magnificently he rose to the height of
his great argument. In the "Moses," wherein
" the forces of nature and of the human con-
science are meant to be typified," he produced a masterpiece of creative art worthy
of the Renaissance in its pregnant simplicity.

The scene represented in this decoration is
one of solemn grandeur. Looming up in the
centre of it is a rocky eminence of tawny
hues, save where a few natural growths bring
some green into the scheme. On the left the
landscape falls as though into an abyss, and
the eye travels over sinister peaks, half veiled
in purple vapors, until a rift in the sky flings
golden light upon the mountain. On the highest plane in the composition Moses kneels, a
rough-hewn, massy, sculptural figure, with
the austere profile of his face partially con-
cealed by arms extended in prayer. This

figure is full of meaning. One is especially
struck by the dignity of the head and the
mute eloquence of the arms and hands. But
the entire body is, indeed, obviously under
the stress of a supernatural emotion. It is easy
to imagine how theatrical or academic it
might have become in the hands of an ordinary painter. With La Farge the skilful handling of form and drapery, admirable in itself,
is, after all, only a means to an end. His main
point is to make us feel that he has portrayed
a great man in a moment of supreme exaltation, and he carries absolute conviction. On
the lower slopes of the mount, the kneeling
figure of Aaron is shown, and, towering
above him, every inch a man, is Joshua, warning the people from the scene. Fire, not in
sharp flames but in rosy billows, gives a
ghastly splendor to the painting. In the
broad blocking out of his composition, and in
the atmosphere communicated to it, La Farge
works on a lofty plane; he is majestic and
sacerdotal, introducing us into a sort of pri-
meval world, where man recognizes in awe
and trembling the nearness of Divinity.

In illustrating "The Relation of the Individual to the State" he took his scene from

that opening book of the "Republic" in which Socrates is represented as engaged in discussion with friends in the circle of Polemarchus. "In this painting," he says in the leaflet already cited, "there has been no strict intention of giving an adequate, and therefore, impossible historical representation of something which may never have happened. But there has been a wish to convey, in a typical manner, the serenity and good nature which is the note of the famous book and of Greek thought and philosophy." Obviously, then, there is no occasion for dwelling on the personal significance, such as it is, of those with whom Socrates is conversing. Details are nothing; the broad idea of Socrates on "the interdependence of man," is everything. Yet in the very moment of reading La Farge's disclaimer of a pedantically historical intention, we are struck, as we raise our eyes to the painting, with a sense of the familiar human reality he has given to something which, as he says, "may never have happened." This is a scene from Plato. It is, as vividly, a scene from Greek life. Plato himself sketches the matter with inimitable realism. When we meet Socrates on the threshold of the "Re-

public," he is not simply the philosopher but
the curious traveller, relishing the delight to
the eye provided by the Bendidean festival.
The incident of his encounter with the man
who wished to hold him in talk is photo-
graphed for us as with a modern camera.
Says Socrates, in Jowett's version: —

"When we had finished our prayers and
viewed the spectacle, we turned in the direction of the city; and at that instant Polemarchus, the son of Cephalus, chanced to
catch sight of us from a distance as we were
starting on our way home, and told his servant to run and bid us wait for him. The servant took hold of me by the cloak behind, and
said: 'Polemarchus desires you to wait.' I
turned round and asked him where his master
was. 'There he is,' said the youth, 'coming
after you if you will only wait.'"

In this passage, and in all that follows to
show how Socrates was prevailed upon to turn
his steps toward the house of Cephalus, we
are carried into the very intimacy of Greek
society, we are conscious of its sights and
sounds, and breathe its bland airs. La Farge
does what Plato does and actually re-creates
for us the beautiful ancient world. Classical

antiquity is not, for him, the cold, skeletonized affair which has satisfied so many "archæological" painters. He brings an architectural motive into his composition in the marble exhedra within whose limits his principal figures are grouped, and, no doubt, in painting Socrates, he was influenced by memories of Greek plastic art. But he portrayed the philosopher and his friends as men first and types of the ancient world afterward. Their easy attitudes are significant of his aim, from those of the three leading figures to the casual, mildly interested pose of the slave girl who leans on the parapet in the foreground. Equally effective in creating a natural impression is the atmosphere in which the whole scene is drenched, an atmosphere borrowing much from the leafage in the background and even more from the landscape filling the distant planes.

The color is superb, handled in many passages with great delicacy, but, on the whole, with a feeling for broad and weighty tones. The masses of light marble in the scene are suffused with a pinkish glow. Above them the dark green of the trees is flecked with tawny tints and beyond, where La Farge recovered

the charioteer of one of his early drawings, the
red tunic of the driver and the white coats of
the horses tell sharply against the greens and
purples of the landscape. The central figure,
one of the listeners, is clothed in red; Socrates
wears a robe in which notes of violet and white
commingle; and his seated friend, to whom he
more particularly addresses himself, is swathed
in draperies of a greenish, bronze-like yellow,
relieved by stuff of a darker hue. The shoulders of a youth who sits with his back toward
the spectator are wrapped in material of tour-
quoise blue and the girl has touches of violet
and gray-white in her dress. The rose color of
the sweetbriar brings still another accent of
sensuous charm into the scene, where a vine
clambers over the exhedra. As a colorist La
Farge adheres to the severe harmony of his
whole plan but everywhere shows his characteristic subtlety and fineness.

It was preëminently in the rôle of a colorist
that La Farge illuminated the big spaces of his
room at St. Paul, but I prefer to terminate
this partial description of the work that he did
there with some remarks on "The Recording
of Precedents," the composition dedicated to
Confucius, as I was privileged to see it in the

cartoon. The cartoon as he used it was not
so much a preliminary study, to be modified
under the influence of mood as the process
of actual painting was carried on, but a true
foundation, prepared for the superimposition
of pigment just as the foundation of a building
is prepared for the walls. If he was a brilliant
colorist he was also a brilliant draughtsman
and a master of design. The Orientals he
brought together in the grove of Confucius
were beautifully drawn at the first stage of
the work and then, as later, their expressions,
attitudes, and relations to one another disclosed
the quality separating the creative artist from
the facile but superficial practitioner of pictorial narrative. The figures were true types
of eastern intellectuality and spirituality and
as they sat absorbed in their devotional work
in a green silence they appealed to me at once
by the intimacy of their grouping and by the
dignity of the spectacle they presented. De-
claring their purpose, not in obvious ways, but
in the indescribable manner signifying a movement of the mind expressed in a movement
of the body, the pose of a head, the play of
a hand, those figures made it plain that they
were engaged upon matters of grave moment.

Though the color was to add so much more its absence was really a benefit to the observer, for in the strokes of charcoal and crayon he could see the very bones of the fabric and the better appreciate La Farge's articulation of them. One could see what an affair of construction a great work of art actually is, how the ultimate glowing picture rests upon a basis of truth rigidly defined. Every tangible factor in the composition was carefully set forth. It was not that the drawing was minutely realistic but rather that the essentials of form which the artist wished to express were grasped with insight and effectively stated. There was no boggling over a difficulty. There were no obscurities anywhere. The elements in the design were simply reduced to their simplest and strongest terms. It was done, moreover, with wonderful breadth, the details being fused together into an imposing whole. The line was full and rich. The modelling had subtlety and power. You felt that the color would come in inevitable sequence, like an integument for a body already having an animated existence.

La Farge was amused by the puzzlement of some of his friends over his mode of work.

They could not always understand his not making quantities of studies in color before he laid out his cartoon, but, as he said to me, the preliminary work in black and white was equally important with that which was to follow. Moreover, in the color stage there were bound to be some modifications, and, said he, "you don't start with your modifications." When he was painting the decoration to which I have just referred he indulged himself in a playful comment on this subject. Confucius is reading from a scroll and on this La Farge got Okakura to help him inscribe in Chinese characters one of the Sage's sayings, "First the white, and then the color on top." He loved to talk about Confucius, whom he had found as interesting as a novel when he was studying him with Okakura's help, and he told me an odd story of what then happened to him. He painted another Confucius in one of the panels which he placed in the Court House at Baltimore and for purely decorative reasons he wanted a perpendicular mass in the centre of it. Finally, he thought of putting a white curtain behind Confucius to shield him from the air as he sat, after his wont, beneath a favorite tree. Okakura, coming in, was greatly astonished at La Farge's scholarship and told him that Confucius had various names, one of them being the Man of the Curtain. But the artist had only been solving a technical problem. He recalled the story of Confucius one day making a little music, as he always did, before he began work. A disciple said to him, "That was not like you; it sounded so cruel." The master replied that he had seen a rat in the grass which a cat had killed, and, said he, "The cruelty got into my music." "There," remarked La Farge, "you have your modern music. What you see and feel, what goes on about you, goes into your work." It is with a sense of his own subjection to that law of human experience that we leave him as a painter, pouring into all that he did the abounding substance of his nature and his life.

VI

GLASS

L A FARGE had the pride of an inventor in his glass. He knew that where that was concerned he had had no predecessors in America, that none of his numerous followers had ever quite rivalled him or was likely to do so, and he knew, finally, that his windows had done more than anything else to spread his fame abroad. One afternoon in Paris I sat with Ary Renan and reasoned with him to the best of my ability, trying to show him that the art of America did not consist, entirely and everlastingly, of the work of those few painters who had expatriated themselves and given away their birthright for a mess of Salon pottage. Of men like Winslow Homer he appeared never to have heard, and of La Farge's pictures and decorations he had only the haziest idea. But he knew all about La Farge's glass; on that point he was quite clear. Had not the French government bestowed the insignia of the Legion of Honor upon the American artist, when he exhibited the Watson Memorial window at the Paris Exposition in 1889? Not content with awarding a medal of the first class to that piece of work the artists of the jury paid him this tribute in their report:

"His work cannot be fully gauged here, where a single window represents a name the most celebrated and widely known in our Sister Republic. He is the great innovator, the inventor of opaline glass. He has created in all its details an art unknown before, an entirely new industry, and in a country without tradition he will begin one followed by thousands of pupils filled with the same respect for him that we have ourselves for our own masters. To share in this respect is the highest praise that we can give to this great artist."

I think that La Farge valued these words and his affiliation to the Legion of Honor above almost any of the numerous other rewards that his career had brought him. In the first place, while the point has nothing to do with the action of the jury, there was in the episode an unspoken recognition of a tie of blood; he liked to feel that officially, in a sense, he was now a Frenchman, too; and then, of course, it was consoling to have his fruitful labors as

The Peacock Window

a pioneer thus ratified before the world at the very focus of the world's artistic endeavors. There was something magisterial about his attitude toward glass, like that of the founder of a great movement in the sphere of purely practical things, or even like that of a commander who had won crucial battles and was thereafter in a position to assert himself. Self-assertion was, to be sure, abhorrent to La Farge's nature, but when he spoke on glass he spoke *ex cathedra* — and he knew it. He spoke and he wrote with some copiousness on the subject and I might proceed at once to cite passages in which he gathered up the threads of experience, but not all of his formal communications had the charm of his intimate speech and accordingly I tell the story of his beginnings in glass very much as he told it to me.

They flowed, he said, from very practical causes. Sometime in the seventies, when he was just back from England, he found that he could not sell his pictures. Durand-Ruel had proposed to exploit his work in Paris and London, looking after his interests much as he had looked after those of Monet and the other Impressionists, sending his pictures to shows, urging them upon collectors, and, in general, "pushing him." The eminent dealer thought that in five years or so he could "make a market" and get for La Farge prices equal to those which he obtained in America, when he sold his pictures at all. The scheme had its advantages, and those not merely of a financial order. To it he owed his first real public triumph. Durand-Ruel had a show in London and hung a landscape of La Farge's, one of his Newport studies, "The Last Valley," between a Rousseau and a Delacroix. It held its own against that stern test. But the artistic success didn't pay bills; at home he was making practically nothing out of his pictures, and so he was much interested when his friend Van Brunt, of the firm of architects, Ware and Van Brunt, proposed his doing one of the windows for Memorial Hall at Harvard.

He was the more in the mood for this venture because, for some five or six months in England, his interest in glass had been stimulated by intercourse with the pre-Raphaelite Brotherhood. He had vivid memories of the band. Burne-Jones was interesting, but there were queer blank walls in his make-up that you bumped your head against. Rossetti was unmistakably the bigger man, much more exciting to know. He made you feel that whether his painting or poetry "came off" or not it was the real thing. La Farge saw, perhaps, more of Ford Madox Brown than of any of the others and preserved a special fondness for him. Brown was peculiarly friendly to the American down to the end of his life. Well, living amongst the pre-Raphaelites and seeing all their enthusiasm over stained glass he was in the very vein to execute Van Brunt's commission. But he could not satisfy himself, and when the window was finished he would not allow it to be put up; he forthwith destroyed it. This was not, however, a confession of defeat. Having got interested he kept at it, despite heart-breaking discouragements. Good glass was almost unobtainable. Powell, an English manufacturer in great vogue, could only send over here a few limited "palettes." And just then the gods smiled. La Farge was in bed, getting over an illness, and pottering with designs of one sort or another, when he glanced at the trifling receptacle on the toilet table containing his tooth-powder, a thing of cheap colored glass, through which, however, at that psychological moment, the light was sending some transforming rays. In an instant he divined immeasurable possibilities and saw ahead of him the opalescent glass which he was before very long to develop. As soon as he got well and on his feet again he looked about him for the means of carrying out his experiments. Over in Brooklyn he ran to earth a Luxembourg glass-maker, with whom he would sit drinking beer and talking until he had got him interested in his plans and committed to a share in them. Thenceforth things went rapidly better and better. Having done over again the big Harvard window for Van Brunt he undertook more work for the same architect, in private houses, and presently made for McKim a window which seemed to put the seal upon all his efforts. This was one for the house of Dr. Richard H. Derby. The pattern in it he took from a carpet in one of the illustrations of the "Hypnerotomachia," borrowing for the purpose from Charles Eliot Norton the rare copy of the book which is now in the possession of Mr. Francis Bullard of Boston. All the architects were surprised at his design, and, to La Farge's huge entertainment, never guessed its Renaissance origin. The window was in

every way a great success and when La Farge
told me this, some three years ago, he still regarded it as one of his best performances. It is
now, by the way, in Dr. Derby's house in
Maine.

By the time he died La Farge had made
several thousand windows, of all sizes and
kinds, little windows that counted as unobtru-
sive notes in decorative schemes and outstanding designs which approximate in scale and in
pictorial interest to the standard he erected
in mural painting. An immense amount of
energy went to the development of this body
of work, which involved not only the produc-
tion of glass and the making of designs but the
training up of a new type of workman and the
incessant supervision of affairs in the shop. It
is not surprising that through some of these
years painting was almost totally abandoned;
but the time came when La Farge not only
took it up again but used his brush on the
large mural decorations we have traversed.
One marvels how a man so frequently broken
down by illness as he was ever contrived to
master the little cosmos in which he lived. It
was, of course, his genius that pulled him
through, his passionate delight in work, so

that fatigue could never wear him down, and
that curious spiritual conviction of having a
mission, an inspiration, and the ability to realize it, which buoys the great artist up and
sustains him where lesser men would fall.

In the all too brief interpretation of La
Farge by Mr. Henry Adams, upon which I
drew in my first chapter, there is a passage
which delicately enforces the predestination of
his friend to greatness in glass, as one taking
up by right a heritage denied to all other
modern craftsmen. They met in Paris in the
fall of 1899, and one of the places they visited together was Chartres, the shrine of the
worker in glass. Mr. Adams thus paints La
Farge in the cathedral whose glory owes so
much to his spiritual forefathers: —

"With the relative value of La Farge's
glass in the history of glass-decoration,
Adams was too ignorant to meddle, and as
a rule artists were if possible more ignorant
than he; but whatever it was, it led him back
to the twelfth century and to Chartres where
La Farge not only felt at home, but felt a sort
of ownership. No other American had a right
there, unless he too were a member of the
Church and worked in glass. Adams himself

was an interloper, but long habit led La Farge to resign himself to Adams as one who meant well though deplorably Bostonian; while Adams though near sixty years old before he knew anything either of glass or of Chartres, asked no better than to learn, and only La Farge could help him, for he knew enough at least to see that La Farge alone could use glass like a thirteenth-century artist. In Europe the art had been dead for centuries, and modern glass was pitiable. Even La Farge felt the early glass rather as a document than as a historical emotion, and in hundreds of windows at Chartres and Bourges and Paris, Adams knew barely one or two that were meant to hold their own against a color-scheme so strong as his."

It was his color again, and even more than in his mural painting, that proclaimed La Farge's authority in glass, his kinship with the old masters; but there was an element in the situation, equally indispensable, which I can only describe as the instinct of the artist for the workshop. He had the craftsman's hand, which must touch and mould substances. When he designed a window he *built* it in the fullest sense of the term. We have noted the

importance he attached to the deeply pon-
dered elaboration of a cartoon for a wall painting. It was the same in his work in glass and
it disappointed him when, even among architects, the fundamental construction of one of
his windows missed appreciation. He sent me
some photographs exhibiting a window before
the stage of color and wrote: "The manner
by which I build a window usually conceals
the inside skeleton and I am often supposed
to begin upside down. Two years ago I had
great difficulty in making one of our best
known architects understand — if indeed he
did understand or believe — that I did not begin my painting by a color sketch, any more
than he did one of his big buildings. Because
I happen to be sensitive to color he supposed
that I must not attend to drawing. It occurred
to me that it might amuse you to see the way
that I begin a window. As you will see, the
whole frame is about constructed and would
almost stand up for itself without any glass,
without any color and with little modelling.
This then is a study of line and is different
from the notion of some of my intellectual
friends that the line is to be put on afterward."

This question of line involved for him, too,

the larger question of an artist's getting his
personality into his work. He could not paint
a picture by the simple process of drawing it
in outline and handing it over to an assistant
to execute. If he sent a design for a window
to the workshop and there left it to take care
of itself he knew that, even under the hands
of the remarkably skilful workmen he had
formed, the essence of his style would evapo-
rate. He knew that by instinct and he knew it
by observation of actual work done in glass.
For a report to the French government written by M. Bing in 1893 he composed some
notes on his experience and practice. At the
outset he emphasizes his belief in the necessity of a close alliance between studio and
workshop:—

"I thought that I had noticed in the work
of the English artists in stained glass that they
had come to the end of their rope, and that
their work in glass had ceased improving, and
it seemed to me that the cause of this was
mainly because the designer had become separated from the men who made the actual
window. I do not mean separated in sympathy
but that they no longer followed the mechanism now that they had learned it, and conse-

quently that whatever they did was only expressed in the manner that had first been used
for their design. Moreover they made designs
for the drawing and not for the result; beautiful drawings — bad result! It occurred to me
that if I made a design for stained glass to be
carried out as was proposed in this country,
that I should follow the entire manufacture,
selecting the colors myself, and watching
every detail."

He did this, and, into the bargain, as I have
previously noted, he moved heaven and earth
to make up for the poverty of material by
which he was confronted. His Luxembourg
glass maker worked under his eye. He imported glass from the European makers. He
built up tones by placing different pieces of
glass in layers and studied the juxtaposition of
different notes of color — an important point,
for the play of light through a window naturally has something like a chemical effect upon
two or more clustered bits of glass, not one in
the cluster escaping modification through the
influence of its neighbor. He dealt with a passage in glass as with one in a painting, devel-
oping countless subtle gradations of color;
and, simultaneously with this pursuit of the

Fruit and Flower Garland

more obvious resources of his craft, he beat
out new methods of holding his composition
together. Not content with giving to his lead
lines a dignity and meaning unknown to his
contemporaries, he devised "a sort of variation
of *cloisonné*, made by joining glass by thin filaments of metal fused to the glass and plated on
both sides with different surfaces of glass ad-
hering." But it is needless to trace all the
ramifications of his technical inventiveness. It
is the character of his glass that counts.

At the roots of that character was La Farge's
understanding of the true office of convention
in art. Convention has for generations suffered
in repute because it has so often been the ref-
uge of the slack intelligence, but to La Farge
it was a precious instrument. Books and photographs were at his hand and he carried in
his brain a kind of anthology of all the decorative styles; but not if he had tried could he
have used them in the wooden, literal way of
the unimaginative artist. His friends had not
divined the source of his pattern in the Derby
window. He baffled them in all his windows.
Wherever he found a motive, his rehandling
of it presently made it very much his own.
And yet, so ingrained was his sense of order

and tradition, that his window might be never so original and still it would admit a certain kinship with historic schools of design. I have in mind, for example, a window for a house in New York in which simulated pilasters, cornice and sill reproduce the carved framework of a window in an old Florentine palazzo. The note of the Renaissance is unmistakable. Between the pilasters in the centre of the window the *clou* of the design is supplied by a mass of flowers and leafage, which it is equally obvious was worked out under the influence of Japanese art. The arrangement, stated in words, suggests incongruity; but the odd thing is that La Farge, through the sheer force of his individuality, completely harmonizes his so different styles, and, what is more, he does so with no concealment of his Italian and Oriental sanctions. Apprehending the thing as a whole you recognize simply his creative faculty. It is only when you coldly analyze it that you see what inspirations he has borrowed— and then you reflect on the rare intuition which led him to borrow those two elements of style and no others.

Formality, which was with him a steadying force, operating from the back of his mind and

never employed for its own sake, entered into
his glass in such wise that while you knew it
to be indispensable there you scarce recognized its presence. His arabesques were not
the dull, insensate devisings of a stodgy geo-
metrician. They were like the pure and beautiful touches of decoration placed sparingly
upon his building by a Greek architect, or like
the nominally negligible cusp, lovingly carved
by the mediæval stonemason on the spire of
a cathedral. They were little knots of form,
meant to hold color in solution; cunningly
wrought webs in which to imprison light.
There are many of La Farge's windows which
therefore seem to be but curtains of jewels
hung between us and the light, pieces of some
new kind of luminous tapestry. The designs
very often are dominated by this merely sensuous spirit; but in many more La Farge showed
his old love for the beauty of flowers, and in
others he used the figure as freely as in mural
painting, and, on occasion, even more auda-
ciously. Courage, indeed, was one of his inborn
traits, and in his work he was ever ready to
press a resource as far as he could make it go.
In glass he felt that the possibilities were illimitable, and, great as his achievements were,
he dreamed of still more daring things.

When he set down his recollections of
Clarence King for the book framed by the
Century Club in honor of that other man of
genius, he described the astounding project
that King talked over with him when the
tomb of General Grant was under considera-
tion. "Our notion," he wrote, "was to have
filled the drum or perhaps even the curves of
the dome with the richest and deepest of
figured glass, built, if I may so express it, into
the walls of the structure, and not a mere fitting in as windows. . . . This imaginary tower
would then have been like the glory of the interior of a great jewel in the day, but at night
would have sent out a far radiance over the
entire city, making as it were a pharos, a
light-house, to be seen from afar by night, as
well as by day, and dominating the river as
well as the land. Of course this was too poetic
and ideal a structure to be accepted at the date
we proposed it." It was not too poetic an ideal
for La Farge, nor would it have been too difficult, too monumental a scheme, for him to
have carried out. On the contrary, as I have
said, in glass nothing could balk him and the
larger the opportunity the more royally he
ruled it. It was as though glass put under his

hand an orchestral body which no
could drive. His notes of color peale
clarion tones, they sank to the mel
murings of the wood-wind, they r
piercing assertiveness of the strings, and then,
again, they were fused in veritably sea-like
waves of power and deep, mysterious beauty.
He put ideas into his windows as he put them
into everything that he did, true religious
emotion in the countless designs that he made
for churches, and an infinite variety of decorative arrangements of form in those produced for secular buildings. But out of the
great mass of his work in glass the masterpiece which I would signalize as most completely representative is the famous Peacock
window, now preserved in the art museum at
Worcester.

This window occupies a place apart. It is,
indeed, something more than a window, and
in that fact lies its exceptional interest. We
are ruled by routine. It is the mission of the
painter to paint; the sculptor is expected to
abide by the rules of plastic art, and, of course,
it is obviously desirable that both artists
should avoid hybrid methods. But is it equally
certain that the man who works in glass

should only make windows; that his art should be governed by a purpose half utilitarian and half decorative? Is there any reason why a design executed in this medium should not exist in and for itself? La Farge answered the question by producing a great work of art for no other reason than that he got endless pleasure out of the manipulation of its materials.

The window — since, for convenience, we must use the term — is an upright panel of modest dimensions, perhaps forty inches high and a little less than half as wide. Filling a good part of the space is a peacock of glorious plumage. The head and body are well up in the higher zone of the composition, so that the colors of the back and of the tail feathers seem to flow as in an iridescent waterfall down toward the watery green background at the bottom. This background, which has a fairly light tone at the base of the design, deepens gradually as it ascends through gradations of dark blues and dark purples. Here and there, on either side of the bird, there is a mass of rosy but quiet color. These episodes are provided by the big peonies which the artist chose for his floral motive. Their lovely

hues are made the lovelier through contrast
with dark leafage. Set within these broader
elements of color is the proud blaze of the
peacock's feathers. They make actually a
kind of conflagration and yet this work is in
nothing more artistic than in its fusion of un-
numbered glowing tints into a positively reposeful harmony. It is as if La Farge had
taken a thousand precious stones and then
filtered the sunlight through them, but had
always remembered so to arrange his jewels,
so to blend or contrast them, that in the en-
semble they should preserve something of the
subtle, sober unity which you find in divers
nominally "gorgeous" things, such as Oriental rugs, the arabesques of the Alhambra,
or ordinary fireworks. In other words, this
is the very poetry of stained glass, a vision of
sensuous loveliness realized in a medium no-
toriously obstinate but made to serve the designer's purpose as readily as pigment serves
it.

I make the allusion to pigment, however,
for the very reason that we must here dis-
tinguish between the two mediums. The Peacock Window is not a picture, an attempt to
do in glass what one might do in paint, an

attempt at translation. On the contrary, its great virtue lies in the fact that it has the character only to be extorted from glass; it expresses the very genius of a medium. You feel this on looking closely into its textures. You see how that marvellous background possesses just the depth and transparency which lie beyond the reach of the brush. You see how the form of the peacock is defined in what I must call "strokes" but that these have a special character, and are not, for example, the equivalents of brush-work; they denote the technique of glass and of glass alone. You see how the thin threads of metal play a part of their own, an indispensable part, toward the unfolding of the charm of the whole. You see, finally, how it was only with glass that La Farge could gain the strength lent by one touch of flaming ruby amid his hues of emerald, sapphire and topaz, or, with tiny apertures at a hundred points, allow the light to sift through like so much diamond dust. It is the kind of work to stir a painter's soul and make him wish to turn from his familiar occupation to experiment in glass. Only, in making the transition, he would have clearly to recognize the fact that he had come

to woo a totally new muse, that while his experience as a painter might help him he would
have to render allegiance to glass as glass,
and observe the full rigor of the game.

That La Farge could do this is one explanation of his preëminence in glass, and with
the thought there must come, I think, an impulse of admiration, passing into reverence,
for the genius and the largeness of soul which
fitted him to conquer so vast an area in the
domain of art. I have spoken of his passion for
work and the store of energy upon which he
valiantly drew, impatient of the claims of
health. "For a sick man I write too much,"
concludes one of the letters quoted in this volume. For a sick man he did too much in every
direction. Nevertheless it is not solely upon
the scale and duration of his physical effort,
perhaps unique in modern times, that the student of his career is moved to reflect, nor upon
his unquenchable enthusiasm, beautiful as that
was. The outstanding trait of La Farge is, of
course, the sheer breadth and richness of his
scope. Versatility is a poor word to apply to
a man of his gifts. It connotes, ordinarily, a
smaller type, a type of powers more lightly
exercised and suffering thereby a certain wan-

ton diffusion of their inner spark. La Farge met the temptation to wreak himself on comparatively minor issues and did not always resist it. When he was working in the Vanderbilt house and making, in the glass for it, some of his most important designs, he took the creation of embroideries there under his care and gave his attention also to some of the woodwork, as he did in the development of his decorative scheme in St. Thomas's Church. Years ago, too, he deviated briefly into sculpture, designing a monument, including a pedestal with steps and a cross, which stands in the cemetery at Newport. But mainly, when he required passages of plastic art in his work, as at St. Thomas's and in the Vanderbilt house, he made the designs and then called in Saint-Gaudens to be his collaborator.

In the arts to which he unreservedly gave himself at one stage or another of his career he saw his inspiration steadily and he saw it whole. You observe the landscapes, flower studies and figure pieces of his early period, the oils, water colors and drawings; you reckon up the paintings of his maturity, the Eastern and South Sea pictures and sketches, and the great mural decorations; and you add to these the stupendous succession of his works in glass. Beneath the surface of it all you perceive a proud and strong spirit holding undistracted to its course, knowing its own mind, confident of its high authority received as through a laying on of hands, and, as in the ancient days, leaving behind it an indelible mark. His multifarious activities are strangely unified by his intrinsic greatness.

VII

THE OLD MASTER

WISDOM was the capstone of his career, the fruition of his long labors — wisdom, and a clairvoyance which made him free of all the real things. If this were a formal biography I suppose I would occupy myself in reciting quantities of external incidents, — the commissions given to La Farge, the medals won, the degrees conferred upon him by learned institutions, and all the other miscellaneous details of a long life. But this is not a formal biography. What I have endeavored to do has been simply to portray the La Farge I knew, a personality, a mind, an artistic force. It is for this reason also that I have refrained from the analysis of scores of works of his, very familiar to me and full of material tempting to discuss. In any case the recording and describing of all of a man's productions is a doubtful enterprise, far more doubtful than we are wont to think, with our modern infatuation for what we are pleased to regard as historical completeness. It is the notion that to be criti-

John La Farge in 1902

cally exhaustive we must count all the leaves
on the tree that explains the frequent preservation of stuff which a great artist would destroy if he knew the moment in which he was
to die. It has been responsible, too, for the
transformation of many a biography into a
wearisome catalogue.

The greatest of artists has his lapses and his
longueurs, not moments merely but days in
which inspiration fails and something like
gaucherie descends upon him. La Farge himself has said that hero worship is not the best
key to understanding. True appreciation of
Whistler, for example, has been seriously ar-
rested in many quarters by the ululations of
the fanatics who would have it that every
touch of a master's hand is priceless. Sometimes it is almost valueless, being without
nervous force or purpose. La Farge knew
well enough that a work of art is not to be
measured by a foot rule and then to be sum-
marily dismissed as good or bad. He knew also
the weight and profound truth of that saying
of Keats: " When I feel I am right, no external praise can give me such a glow as my own
solitary reperception and ratification of what
is fine." Writing to me of a new window that

he had completed, and that "in the shop looks handsome," La Farge goes on to say: "It is of a novel idea, I think, and a new treatment — in our part of work — but *the main point is that I like it*." The italics are mine. I use them as a reminder of what it is always important to look for in his, or in any artist's work — what he intended and achieved, not what we think he ought to have done. But it is with a sense of La Farge's own outlook upon questions of this sort that I have refused to write of him as of a demigod. I should be sorry if from any of the foregoing chapters the reader had surmised that I wished to paint him as impeccable and possessed of the unanswerable authority of a force of nature. No man of genius that ever wielded a brush has been so fearful a wildfowl as all that.

It is enough if we recognize that La Farge at his best produced certain works of art of a gem-like perfection. The "Paradise Valley" is one of these and there are other landscapes, dating from the same period, which I would rank with it. Many of his flower paintings and figure pieces are on the same plane. The "Ascension," amongst his mural decorations, and the "Peacock Window" in the field of

glass, are there to illustrate again the consummate master. But the whole trend of my
study has been toward the exposition of his
essential greatness as an artist and I need not
labor the point. What is necessary to the fuller
realization of his character, the closer grasp
of the special quality of his genius, is a sense
of that complexity on which we cannot too
often pause, that dependence of his upon
mental and spiritual mood, that protean habit
which, if it prevented him from invariably
striking twelve, made every movement of his
forces an affair of subtly personalized interest.
He was not the painter to brood over a work
in every instance until he left it an example
of rounded perfection, then going on to ab-
sorption in a similar task, so that his life was
a succession of so many flawless milestones.
He took things in his stride. He never scamped
anything; but there was always a tremendous
ferment going on in his brain, he was always
interested in many things and subject to gusts
and jets of emotion and curiosity. Hence, in
the vast body of his work, the presence of
quantities of things which, from the point of
view of the schoolmaster distributing marks
of merit and demerit, are not, strictly speak-

ing, masterpieces, but which have his quality
in them, and, above all, are intensely original.
I cannot lay too heavy a stress upon the absence from his work of traits linking him, as
an imitator, with any masters or schools of the
past. In his own time he had only two paral-
lels, Watts and Moreau, and he was more
purely the artist than either of them. Like
Tintoretto, who sought to blend the color of
Titian with the form of Michael Angelo, the
English artist deliberately sat down to conscious emulation. He paid the penalty in a certain exaggerated subjection to tradition. Also
there was forever lurking in him a Tolstoyan
ambiguity as to where the claims of art and
those of morals were to be differentiated. La
Farge never fell into either mistake. He began
without formulas and with a distrust of their
efficacy; he ended in the same mood of detachment from them, with the same distrust.
Though tradition and morals were both ever
present in his conception of life and of art he
kept each in its place. He thought too accu-
rately to be misled in these matters, and on the
side of technique, which is so closely allied to
them in the genius of a man of mind, he knew
too well just what he was about. It is amusing

to compare him with Moreau. In the sphere
of imagination there was a tie of sympathy
between them, but where the Frenchman
missed the beauty of painted surface in spite
of striving for it, he, as I have shown in an
earlier chapter, got it easily enough when he
tried for it. When we miss it in his later period
we recognize a renunciation, not a depriva-
tion.

I must speak again of his mixed feeling on
this point. At times he would regard his detachment from the manipulation of pigment
and the "bloom" to which I have alluded, as
a regrettable sacrifice imposed by hard cir-
cumstance. In the reminiscences he wrote for
me there is a passage almost plaintively expressing this point of view. Referring to his
decorative work, he says, "In all this there is
a good deal of fun, but I still regret that I
gave up the art of painting, for which I had,
evidently, quite a talent and for which I had
made very serious studies, many far in advance of the people of my day." Nevertheless, as he constantly made plain to me, he
did not exaggerate the significance of the art
of painting as it was illustrated in his earlier
manner. He simply recognized the fact that

there are kinds of painting. It is hard, as I have shown, for many modern artists to seize this truth. It was simple enough for La Farge, with his capacity for infinite degrees of adjustment. Simple enough for him, I say, yet for the biographer, striving to trace the windings of his thought, the reasoning by which he arrived at his resolutions and reconciled all the warring impulses met on the way, every stage of analysis involves new obstacles. Years of intimacy with La Farge could not make him less baffling, less elusive. In the first chapter of this book I have quoted the remarkable analysis of his genius by his old friend and travelling companion, Henry Adams. Here, from a private letter, are some further passages from the same hand : —

"I am such a matter-of-fact sort of person that I never could try to approach La Farge from his own side. He had to come over to mine. Yet he, like most considerable artists, worked so much more intuitively than intellectually that he could not have taught me much, had he tried; because I could only work intellectually. For that reason I thought I could follow him best in his glass, where his effects were strong and broad. Although I thought him quite the superior of any other artist I ever met, — and I have no special reason for limiting the remark to artists alone, — he was so 'un-American,' — so remote from me in time and mind, — and above all, so unintelligible to himself as well as to me, that I have preferred to talk little about him, in despair of making him or his art intelligible to Americans; but if I did try to do it, I would rather try by putting some of his glass side by side with that of other centuries back to the twelfth. Perhaps, by that means, he might become intelligible.

"He was a marvel to me in his contradictions. Unlike most men of genius he had no vices that I could detect. He had one of the most perfectly balanced judgments that could ever exist. Towards me, he seemed always even-tempered to an inconceivable degree. I do not mean benevolent, or sentimental, or commonplace, but just *even*, and in his disapproval as well as in his acceptance. Of course he was often severe, but his severity itself was shaded and toned. Yet he was not easy to live with, thus contradicting even his contradictions.

"The task of painting him is so difficult as

to scare any literary artist out of his wits. The thing cannot be done. It is like the attempt of the nineteenth-century writers to describe a sunset in colors. Complexity cannot be handled in print to that degree. La Farge used to deride his own attempts to paint sea and sky and shadow in the South Seas, and was rather fond of pointing out how, at a certain point of development, he always failed, and spoiled his picture. At a certain point of development, the literary artist is bound to fail still more because he has not even color to help him, and mere words only call attention to the fact that the attempt to give them color is a predestined failure. In the portrait of La Farge you must get not only color, but also constant change and shifting of light, as in opals and moonstones and star-sapphires, where the light is in the object. You need to write as an artist, for artists, because the highest-educated man or woman of the world cannot comprehend you, if you qualify and refine, as La Farge did, and then contradict your own refinements by flinging great masses of pure force in your readers' faces, as he did in his windows."

The hope that lures one on in this struggle to qualify and refine, to find unity in com-

plexity, is a hope that sustains the student
of every great character. Most men of eminence leave behind them the memory of a
controlling principle, visible like some still,
central flame, shining through the bulk of
their achievement. Call it what you will, —
the ruling passion, the influence of an environment, the force of an idea, — you know the
man for a type, and, no matter how averse you
may be from classifying genius, you inevit-
ably because instinctively give it its label. The
mere convenience we automatically seek in
our mental transactions leads us to put a great
man in his group, to think of him under a given
head in the history of human endeavor. This
one, we say, was constructive; that one was
an agent of broad imaginative inspiration; another we call a moral aid, and still another is
a voice of doubt. The list of tags is endless, but
that fact does not discourage our use of tags.
I use the expression, of course, in no narrow
sense, but as it applies in our dealings with
even the greatest men. When I ask myself,
following this habit, what La Farge preëminently stood for, I find something trivial and
misleading in the association of his genius with
anything that connotes a style, a school. Into

what definitely bounded category could we force the artist whose character I have attempted to analyze? But in his rejection of formulas there lies, I think, a clue. To pursue, as far as one may, the secret of that love of freedom that moved him all his life long, is to approach what I believe to be his distinguishing trait, the one giving us our label—if label we must have.

La Farge's ruling passion, perceptible as we see his life as a whole and perhaps only then —though it is revealed by flashes in his talk and writings— was the lust of knowledge. He loved knowledge for its own sake. To the thinking man knowledge is a kind of sensation —it is tangible, sensuous, thrilling, a thing as grateful to his whole being as is the sharp salt savor of the sea, cold, stinging, and ineffably delicious when it is breasted naked on a burning day. To such a man the acquirement of knowledge is an affair of unceasing zest and pleasure. And to such a man this perpetual hunt through the world of thought is nothing if not disinterested; it means nothing if it does not mean the development in his soul of a profound humility. I see La Farge questioning, always questioning, but never suffering disap-

pointment because the solution of his problem
was always just beyond his reach. He would
have been disappointed, in a sense, if he could
have grasped it. That would have spelled
finality and would have taken too many surprises, too many illusions, out of life. Hence,
too, the liberality of his judgments, his refusal
to regard any question as settled, or any personality, historic or in his own time, as conclusively understood and explained. His respect for the individuality of any man, great
or small, lay deep and, I may even say, had
about it something of gentleness, of tenderness. He feared to misunderstand, to misjudge.

There was always the other side of the
medal to be accounted for. What was it like?
He hungered to know. But to get the knowledge he used all the discretion imaginable and
when it was his he was doubly anxious to treat
it with respect, to be quite sure. The new
knowledge did not round out, any more than
it cancelled, the old. It only complicated the
original question — and thereby made it the
more delightful. He was a Heracleitean. He
saw life in a flux and that gave it, for him, its
charm. The most La Fargesque saying I know
occurs in a letter written in sickness and noting

how an invalid necessarily disturbs all the people around him. "I stood as well as I could,"
he says, "the annoyances I inflicted." In that
remark, absolutely accurate, sincere, and characteristic, there is perfectly mirrored his in-
ability to see only one side of a question, his
completely disinterested interest in both sides
of it.

He was so accustomed to thinking and feeling in this way that in spite of a pretty broad
experience of human nature he was apt to
take for granted the same elasticity of mind
in others. Naturally he knew, from time to
time, rather startling disillusionment. This
always puzzled and grieved him a little, for he
deplored what seemed to him a violation of the
proper laws of thought, and, besides, he hated
the misunderstandings so often promoted by
such violation. Misunderstanding leads to
anger and bitterness. La Farge was not a
quarrelsome man and he deprecated these
evils as he would have deprecated the invasion
of his studio by ugly noises. Moreover, the
importance sometimes attached to the little
troubles of life outraged his sense of proportion. He delighted in Cellini, loving best of all
his naturalness, and it annoyed him that peo-

ple often got excited about the Italian's truth
or falsehood. Speaking of this, one night, he
tried to recall some "clever" person who had
been guilty of the unfairness, and then said,
with a laugh, "But why try to remember stupid, unpleasant things?" For one thing, he
felt that such remembrance not seldom ended
in complete misrepresentation. It amused him
to reflect on the manner in which he had himself occasionally suffered from heedless gossip,
and in a late letter he asked me : —

"Do you remember the old story —
French — absolutely true, I was told, in the
French office? An employé finds a good deal
of money in big bills. Brings it in to office. Is
thanked. A few years after, is mentioned for
advancement. The 'Ministre' in charge of
office says, 'But why? I remember his name.
Was he not implicated in an affair about money
found? No proof against him — perhaps?'"

He told me that story apropos of another,
which had been told about himself, one possibly familiar to some of my readers, for a man
like La Farge is always the subject of anec-
dotes handed about. It had to do with an
Oriental rug which he had purchased years
ago in Boston, at a time when, in the opinion

of persons having nothing whatever to do
with it or with him, the purchase was immea-
surably extravagant. Well, it was a Mecca
carpet — some five feet square — for which
La Farge paid the sum of forty dollars ! And
his crime consisted in buying the piece from
under the nose of some one else who wanted
it. Recollecting the insignificant episode with
much enjoyment of its drollery, he wrote me
of the odd connection between this rug and a
decorative problem which he had to carry out
at the time in consonance with certain "de-
nominational" principles : —

"The 'motives' of it are on the ceiling of
the Congregational Church in Newport. Now
my rug had struck me as solving the problem
of the ceiling and part of the wall. It suggested
some of the earlier Romanesque in cruciform
patterns, and yet was evidently not a 'Rom-
ish' pattern. I dare not say it was Mahom-
medan. So you see the careless, spendthrift,
bad man had some close idea of business duties in his wild career."

There is an old tale about the great Duke
of Wellington, ruefully murmuring that he
was "much exposed to authors." La Farge
was much exposed to committees. I think he

Waterfall in our Garden at Nikko, Japan

liked them, or at any rate that they had for him a kind of dark fascination, as of august bodies whose *terribilità* might at any moment drift into an amusing phase. There is, to be sure, something about committees that is not wholly solemn. From the member of shrinking modesty, who knows nothing about art but "knows what he likes," to the member who does n't know even that, and is accordingly, like Habakkuk, *capable de tout*, they are all, in the nature of things, possessed of a demon. I do not recall if in that amusing book of M. Le Bon's on "The Psychology of the Crowd," which I read long ago, there is a chapter on committees, but if there is one it must account for their ways on mystic grounds. No doubt committees, and individuals, occasionally thought that they had reason to be vexed with La Farge. There is, of course, something heinous in an artist's failure to finish and deliver a piece of work, according to contract, on a given Wednesday afternoon at half past two. But sometimes one wearies of the hypothesis that the business man is the only respectable type in an imperfect world, whose orderliness, punctuality, solvency, and unassailable rectitude must excite our blind vene-

ration. For my own part, over the anguish of
the owners of those Brahminical toes on which
La Farge may have reposed himself from
time to time, I cannot weep salt tears. On the
contrary, I contemplate it with that emotion
sanctioned in one of La Rochefoucauld's best
remembered maxims. After all, a great artist
is not necessarily supplied with all the virtues
of a stockbroker or a manufacturer. And to
any one who really knew La Farge it was
plain that he longed to keep his affairs in apple-
pie order. It was not easy to do this, with his
ill-health and with the mountains of work that
he had to get through, but his good faith was
inextinguishable, as was his desire to meet the
wishes of those with whom he had dealings
and to share with them the sweets of goodwill. We used often to talk about his adven-
tures in the world of everyday business, where
practical considerations rise up like ravening
wolves in the path of the artist eager to realize
his dreams. Writing to me on this subject he
once said : —

"You can hardly imagine how absurd it is
to realize that you cannot give certain extra
folds to a cloak because they will cost so many
dollars more, or that an extra angel's head is

worth seventy-two dollars and must be cut out, or one of its hands hidden because that is five dollars, and that the very shape of the fold is a matter of money. So that which of the business firms of England, or, indeed, of the United States, has the deepest religious sentiment, I do not know.

" Perhaps you will remember that in one of my lectures at the Metropolitan Museum I recorded how some good women, some nuns, consulted me on this question. I advised them to take the young man with the prettiest beard and the sweetest cravat, whom I think they would have taken anyhow. This is funny but it is absolutely true. The same good ladies did not like the old Italian paintings, from A to Z, which I had shown them to get an idea of what they liked and to help their tastes a little. These are the foundations on which we build for Eternity."

The passage is good-natured. La Farge had exemplary patience with the difficult conditions often confronting him. He knew that Rome was not built in a day and he was slow to complain. Upon a memorable occasion he spoke out with electrifying effect. When, in January, 1909, at a dinner given by the

Architectural League of New York, that body
bestowed upon him its medal of honor for the
best work of decorative painting shown at its
exhibition that year, he remarked in his speech
of acceptance that a certain firm of architects
had not, for twenty years, given him any work
to do. Of course this made a sensation in the
newspapers of the next morning and early I
received a hurried note, saying, "Oh, why
were you not at the dinner of the League last
night? 'They' had the most stupid account in
some of the papers of what I may have said —
so inaccurately reported as to make me seem
to attack persons and things." He was cruelly
distressed, and a little later there came in
the *Tribune* this explanation of the spirit in
which he had spoken : —

"I am simply voicing my regret at the lack
of coördination between the arts — between
the mural painters and the architects. We
were all friends at the dinner and knew each
other well. As for my statement that McKim,
Mead & White had refused to give me any
work, that was based on something the late
Stanford White said to me. We were intimate friends; yet he remarked to me once
that for business reasons he could never have
me do any work. Why, I do not know.

"As for the medal presented to me, when I said that I received it with 'some reticence of thanks,' I meant simply that I was getting to that time of life when such things meant little. At my age one thinks more of the heaven in 'Andrea del Sarto' — how does it go? well, never mind — it's fifty-two years since I've read it. But it is about painting within the four walls of heaven with Michael Angelo and the others."

The incident was characteristic of La Farge in a certain innocent, faun-like mischievousness, and even more in its illustration of what I have already touched upon, his readiness to assume that others could look, as he could, all around a subject. There was no malice in that outburst of his and I may appositely recall the fact that when McKim died he placed in my hands, to publish in the *Tribune*, a long letter on the architect full of loyalty and the most affectionate appreciation. Misunderstanding and ill-feeling were, I must say once more, hateful to him. I remember that when the Society of American Artists was to go back into the fold of the Academy of Design he asked me to come to the dinner with which the event was to be celebrated, and expressed

his fear of there being any ill-timed comment on the subject anywhere. Fearful that
the newspapers might not be entirely sympathetic in their reports of the occasion, he
said to me: "We can't have anything too
quiet, even to the extent of there being nothing. This is all the more because many of
our younger people would like to have heads
broken and a general scrimmage, and what
for I don't know." It might seem, perhaps,
irrelevant to speak of these trifles that have
gone down the wind, but La Farge was a man
of genius, and in consequence people sometimes found him "difficult." I like therefore
to show how really lovable he was and how
careful at bottom for the interests and feel-
ings of others. In all our long friendship I
never once knew him to be unfair or un-
kind. To me he seemed always as he seemed
to Mr. Adams, "even-tempered to an inconceivable degree." One more testimony to the
fineness of his spirit I wish to cite, for I know
that it gave him deep pleasure. The great
decoration in the Church of the Ascension
suffered delay in being carried to completion. Something of what he told me about it I
have set down earlier in my narrative, and, in-

deed, it is unnecessary to traverse the subject
in detail. There were stories again, like that
about the rug, only in this case they showed
him as sorely trying the patience of his committee. They wounded him, for they were un-
deserved, and the late Dr. E. W. Donald, who
had been Rector of the Church of the Ascension when the work was done, wrote to him a
letter from which I take the following:—

"Perhaps you won't be sorry to have me
say in black and white that in all the dealings
I have had with you (and as I look back upon
them they have been many and important)
there has been absolutely nothing that could
by even a wicked ingenuity be twisted into the
semblance of anything other than honorable
dealing. To be sure, my lay ignorance of the
ways in which an artist works has made it
possible for me to be exasperated at delays,
but completion of the work has invariably
wholly removed exasperation, because, after
completion, even I could recognize that delay
meant the enhancement of the artistic value
of the work. Indeed, as I look back upon the
years in which you were at work upon the
great painting in the Ascension, and shame-
facedly recall my clumsy and perhaps brutal

attempts to hurry you, I am filled with contrition. The soiled and ragged and crumpled curtain has long since vanished from my memory, and the great painting alone occupies the field of view. Perhaps, you, too, as you look back upon our relation have found it possible to forgive the pragmatic priest for his unreasonableness, recognizing that it was due, not to personal animosity, but to crass ignorance of the artist's life. At all events, as I think to-day of our coming window in Trinity, I find myself entirely able to wait with exemplary patience for its coming, knowing that delay means greater beauty in the glass. How much more reasonable we grow about big things as we advance in age! How much more space in one's life the heart occupies! I frankly confess that with each year I find, alongside of my ever increasing admiration for your work as an artist, a corresponding increase of affection for you as a man and friend; so that to-day, instead of looking upon you, as years ago I used to, solely as the great artist who makes our churches beautiful, I now think of you as the friend of my youth and of my manhood, to whom I owe much, apart from the debt your artistic work lays me under."

There were many who owed him much, especially amongst the artists of his time. Some of them he taught, but it is not so much the training that he gave his pupils and assistants that I would emphasize. It is, rather, the broad stimulus that he added to their lives, the spur they got from him, apart from mere questions of technique. Many years ago Saint-Gaudens worked with him, on the sculptural part of the decoration at St. Thomas's Church, and only death terminated their friendship. In the fall of 1903 the sculptor wrote to him and in the course of his letter said : "Later on I picked up 'McClure's,' where your articles on Millet, Rousseau, and Corot made the same impression that your work and my relations with you have always made and inspired in me to do the right and big thing." That was the nature of La Farge's influence. He founded no school. His work was inimitable and he would not have imposed his style upon any one, even if he could have done so. But just as certain of his followers came to understand form and color the better for his example and teaching, so, I believe, these artists and a generation both of artists and of laymen came insensibly to profit by the largeness and rich substance of his ideas. His work exerted a spiritual force. It refined taste and fostered imagination. It made powerfully for the establishment of a high ideal. And not only his work as an artist did this; he helped his time through his personality, through his talk, and through his participation in the organizing actions of his fellow artists. You did not find La Farge on the jury in every exhibition, but you found him working in his quiet way for every good cause. I have mentioned his letter on McKim. "Suddenly one night," he wrote, "the all-powerful Daniel Burnham dropped into the Century from Chicago, anxious to persuade McKim, whom he could not wake or find. We called on Mr. Cadwalader, who could help, and Mr. McKim was persuaded to listen to the plan of laying out Washington according to the ancient schemes, and also evidently new ones to come. There it was. And almost the next day the whole party went down to take hold of the future. The painter, myself, dropped out later because painters come in afterward in the modern methods. In the ancient ways they were called upon to make great cities, such cities as Florence, but it was a beautiful thing to do and the memory of this with Mr. Burn-

ham and our dear Saint-Gaudens remains." In
such ways his devotion to the artistic welfare
of the country never failed. And when he was
not thus serving his period the transmission of
his ideas went forward through his books.

There are too many of La Farge's own
words in this volume for any minute exposition of his purely literary traits to be required,
but there are one or two observations on the
subject which may fairly be made. He wrote
as he painted and drew, and as he talked —
from the impulse toward self-expression which
is characteristic of the creative genius. "There
is no such thing," says Swinburne, "as a dumb
poet or a handless painter. The essence of an
artist is that he should be articulate." For a
man so naturally meditative La Farge was curiously impelled to be articulate, to give forth
the thoughts constantly crowding upon him,
and if he could not be making a work of art or
conversing he was apt to take up the pen. He
was an extraordinarily assiduous writer of letters. He enjoyed writing them, and, by the
way, he liked publication. Alluding to a note
in which he had corrected some misstatement
in a newspaper, he wrote to me, "It is amusing
to be in print and I can realize the joy of battle

of so many in the wars of the press." He wrote
with such good will and so voluminously that
by and by his calligraphy showed the strain.
The hand, often exhausted with painting, could
scarce keep pace with the exhaustless brain,
and although, even in the last weeks of his life,
he could with pen or pencil give beautiful form
to a letter when he took the time, for years his
delicate handwriting flowed almost too swiftly
across the page and was not infrequently difficult to decipher. Miss Barnes has told me of a
quaint episode due to this illegibility. He had
written a letter to the late J. Q. A. Ward and,
on receiving a reply a day or two later, found
it impossible to make it out. Meanwhile he
had forgotten just what he had wanted to discuss with his friend, but feeling vaguely that
it was something important he contrived to get
a message sent to Ward which brought him
to the studio. After a little while La Farge
remarked, casually, that he had received the
reply to his letter but perhaps it had been
written in haste, and, in any case, he could n't
quite get at its contents. "Oh," said Ward,
with a laugh, "I merely wrote to say that I
could n't make out a word of your letter!"

Partly because of the mere physical bother

— and the delay — involved in writing clearly,
and even more because it suited his temperament, La Farge took to dictation, and, in later
years especially, his literary work as well as
much of his private correspondence was done
with the aid of a stenographer. The practice
was favorable to the preservation of all that
was most characteristic in his mental habit.
It made the reader of a book of his, or of a
letter, the surer of his gleams of subtle suggestion, of his parenthetical excursions, of
his eloquent pauses. In the letter from which I
have previously quoted, Mr. Adams says : —

"He wrote as he talked, so that you have
his conversation almost exact in his writings.
I used to think that if he were stenographically
reported, we should find only multiplied forms
of expression. In these he was, as you know,
very abundant, and his choice of words and
figures very amusing, so as to put him among
the best talkers of the time, if not actually the
first, as I thought he was; but the charm of
talk is evanescent and largely in voice and
manner. Except in cases where a certain
forced brutality occurs, as in Dr. Johnson, or
in Whistler, reports of table-talk are apt to
disappoint; and La Farge's tones were too

shadowy to bear forcing. I think his letters
from Japan repeat his table-talk much better
than any memory could recall it."

Analysis of La Farge as a writer leads to
one discovery which brings us sharply back
to his character as a man. At the outset of my
study I glanced at his faculty for the avoidance of those things which he did not want to
do. Conversely, when La Farge wanted to do
a thing he could do it, and this fact is vividly
disclosed by certain of his writings. He was
wont, as Mr. Adams says, to write as he
talked, and accordingly there are pages of his
— such as those, for example, in his book of
lectures, "Considerations on Painting"— in
which you must follow him with very great
care. His prose there is close packed, sometimes almost to the point of density. Thought
treads fast upon the heels of thought, and one
nuance melts into another. He is not obscure,
but he is so full and rich that one must needs
walk warily, for fear of missing a subterra-
nean drift. On the other hand, when La Farge
chose to be, I will not say didactic, but the
more or less practical narrator, he could make
his writing the easiest reading in the world.
Turn to his book of "Great Masters," in

which he traverses the lives and works of
Michael Angelo, Rembrandt, Hokusai, and
three or four other commanding types. In
that book he proves himself a *vulgarisateur* of
artistic knowledge in the best meaning of the
term, the true colleague of those men of taste
and learning who have made the French text-
book a model. He draws all the essential
threads of information and of criticism into his
hands, and, while it never occurred to him to
"write down" to his readers, he knew how so
to humanize his subject, how so to clarify and
to simplify it, as to render it delightful to the
least instructed layman. In a measure, I think,
this effect was consciously secured — he knew
his task and executed it with deliberate intent.
But also it is well to note that amongst La
Farge's many and complex traits there were
those of the exact student, the conscientious
and orderly thinker. We must remember, too,
his trained and tireless vision. Nothing escaped
him ; and if, as I am always recalling, he made
unerringly for the thing that counted, it was
also characteristic of him to give their full
value to details possibly seeming, to some
eyes, negligible. Following him upon his
travels in the South Seas or in the East, you

might take him for a disciple of Taine in his predilection for the "little facts" to which that philosopher attached so much importance in the appraisal of a people. I might illustrate this by citations of his notes on tribal customs and the like in the Pacific islands, but that would divert us somewhat from the particular point in hand, which is La Farge's technique as a writer. For the illumination of that I prefer to choose one of those passages which he liked to affix to the titles of his pictures in an exhibition catalogue. With one of the loveliest of his Japanese paintings, "The Fountain in our Garden at Nikko," he used to give this extract:—

"We have a little fountain in the middle of the garden, that gives the water for our bath, and sends a noisy stream rolling through the wooden trough of the wash room. The fountain is made by a bucket placed upon two big stones, set in a basin, along whose edge grow the iris, still in bloom. A hidden pipe fills the bucket and a long green bamboo makes a conduit for the water through the wooden side of our house. With another bamboo we tap the water for our bath. In the early morning I sit in the bathroom and paint this little pic-

ture, through the open side, while A., upstairs
in the veranda, is reading in Dante's 'Paradise' and can see, when he looks up, the great
temple roof of the Buddhist Mangwanji."

The number of nouns in this brief description, and the straightforward manner in which
they are made to build up the picture, suggest
for a moment the strictly realistic writer. All
through his notes of travel La Farge keeps his
eye on the object and is meticulously faithful
to its every detail. His impressions, essentially
atmospheric, rest upon the firmest of foundations. The passage just cited illustrates this
point and it shows, too, what clarity of style
was accessible to him when he was in the mood
to secure it. Paradoxically, the mood came,
so to say, at call, or, in other words, he instinctively fitted his style to the occasion. It
was the true envelope of his thought, subtle
when the latter took a metaphysical turn, and
simplicity itself in a familiar record like the
foregoing. Again we think of his possession
of "one of the most perfectly balanced judgments that could ever exist." It served him
unfailingly, directed his every touch and enabled him to regard every question in the right
perspective. He had the sanity, which is to say

the common sense, of genius. We may see this
further operating in still another phase of his
thought.

La Farge's attitude toward the whole question of the criticism of art was very much that
of the mature master who is also a man of the
world. Like every man of genius he went his
way untroubled by external admonition; he
knew he could trust the still small voice of his
own instinct. But the intellectual nature of his
artistic habit made him fully appreciative of
the importance of criticism as criticism, and
he had not the smallest trace of that jealousy
of the writing profession which characterizes
so many artists and has its most famous ex-
emplar in Whistler. If he realized, with that
gay dogmatist, that art is art and mathematics
is mathematics, it did not keep him from recognizing the value of a penetrating thought
wherever he found it. He read with intense
sympathy what painters have said about their
art, he read Delacroix and Fromentin, — and
Whistler, too, — but then he read everything,
and he would have scorned to reject the sound
saying of a layman just as he would have
smiled, as, indeed, I have known him to smile,
over the naïve hypothesis that any artist, by the

simple process of being an artist, may brevet
himself an oracle of artistic wisdom. Such wisdom draws its validity and force from the individual, and it has a way of cropping up in the
most diverse places. For scholarship, especially of that scientific sort which has arisen in
the last half-century to correct the wilfulness
and steady the principles of impressionistic
criticism, he had the respect which he yielded
to every manifestation of honest thought, but
he did not share in the fond belief that there
is something sacrosanct about it. I have from
Brander Matthews an amusing story of La
Farge on our latter-day craze for the connoisseurship which wreaks itself on puzzles of
attribution. They were talking at the dinner
table about the Morellian hypothesis and La
Farge said :—

"Let us suppose the testing of a picture of
my own some time many years hence. The
Morelli of the future might look at it narrowly
and after a while conclude that the hands and
eyes in the picture showed a Japanese conception of form. He would remember that I
had kept a workshop, a *bottega*, after the old
Italian fashion, and he would have heard that
I had had Japanese people with me. So he

would say that the picture was a studio piece,
the work of a Japanese assistant. Then the
Berenson of that day would come along and
look it all over very carefully and get much
interested in the spirituality of the face. He
would say that there was something very soft,
very feminine, about it and he would wind up
by attributing it to Miss So-and-So, another
pupil. — But it would be a La Farge, all the
same."

He had scholarship himself, but he was more
than modest about it, and, though he did not
distrust his judgment, he was never inclined
to make too much of it or to lay down the law.
He told me of a visit he once paid to the house
of a collector who possessed an antique head,
on which he wanted La Farge's opinion. In
examining the thing, he said, he knew perfectly well that he was not bringing into play
the tremendous apparatus of the "expert."
"But," he went on, "there was something
about it. I remembered many things that I had
often seen abroad — and I felt quite sure that
it was one of those pieces of the late eighteenth
or early nineteenth century, when the sculptors in France were doing things very like the
antique. Perhaps some one had just tried his

hand at an imitation. I do not know. But I do
not think it was really ancient Greek." The
whole impression that La Farge gave me in
this episode was that of a man who knew his
ground and had his inner conviction but abhorred flat assertion and, moreover, was hum-
bly willing to be convinced that he was wrong.
Vehement assertion would have jarred him,
would have wounded his sense of the subtleties of things and of the impossibility of giving
to matters of art the hard, fixed outline of matters of fact. And "attribution," with a good
deal else belonging to the great mass of scientific paraphernalia, could not interest him
overlong. With his artist's passion for intrinsic
beauty such things sank for him more or less
into the background. He saw the peril they
involve of luring one away from the fundamental things and of importing the spirit of
dissension into the still air of delightful studies.
Criticism, for him, was one of the gentlest of
arts, and it was characteristic of him, by the
way, to be most careful of its use amongst
his contemporaries. He could never be persuaded to criticise the works of his fellow artists and I never knew him to disparage one
of them.

His insistence upon the main issue, the question of sheer beauty, regardless of the origin of a work, was manifest in his experience as a collector. He assembled quantities of works of art in his time, especially works from the East, and he bought them with knowledge, as those familiar with his collections well know; but when he acquired a thing it was because he found it beautiful and loved it, and for no other reason. In 1908, when he disposed of some of his possessions at auction, he wrote this, when it was all over, to Mr. James Huneker: —

"Let me say that I liked your reference to my sale — to me unfortunate — but things have sold badly and sales have no souls. I have never been a collector for every reason — and one principal one — that study is not in that way — and even influences one wants. I went to Yamanaka's a little while ago with two books to ask their value. I was told at once six or seven hundred dollars for one — the other *none* whatever. And yet the one without price was the one I look at occasionally to feel the breath of poetry blow free. But it had *no duplicate* to compete with it — was unknown to trade. Some of my things, but

Official Presentation of Gifts of Food — Samoa

very few, I had long. It is just fifty years ago
that I bought my first Hokusai book — imagine the joy of first discovery. So I lit off and
I have had my likings for Japan. In fact, I
know of no artists before me. My French
people laughed at me for 'Les amours exo-
tiques.' But here people thought moral ill of a
lover of Jap art — as for the lover of Blake or
Goya. I think I still have the bad name —
tho' I parted with the objects, almost all, some
forty years ago."

He had discriminated from the beginning.
It was with a critical mind that he had made
his first European travels. Have we not seen
how, even as a lad in the studio of Couture,
he used an exacting judgment and weighed
his problems in a delicate balance? More and
more as the years went on he came to rest
upon first principles, to go only for that which
he knew to be broad and lasting. His curiosity was insatiable. For example, he delighted to tell how on a visit to Venice he had
contrived to get hold of a forger of pictures
and had studied with him long enough to
learn all the secrets of the trade. But curiosity never carried him off his feet, and he
seemed almost uncannily immune from those

enthusiasms which so often disturb an artist's
poise. More than once in our conversations
some type of decadence would come up. Nothing could have been more instructive than
his talk then. If the painter in question had
any merits at all, no matter how slight, La
Farge invariably brought them to the surface,
and not even the worst sinner was carelessly
or harshly dismissed. But gently, and often
with a kindly humor, the man would be definitely put in his place. You felt, when La
Farge had finished, that above all things he
had been just. I must cite here some passages
from a letter of his written to Mr. Adams
about Gauguin, the "Post-Impressionist,"
whose sojourn in the South Seas predisposed
La Farge to take an interest in his work: —

"I forget everything more and more. I
am therefore not quite certain that you are
absolutely and entirely in the wrong about
that wild Frenchman's being in Tahiti. I
say 'wild Frenchman'—I should say stupid
Frenchman. I mean Gauguin.

"No, I think that he went there just as we
arrived in Paris in 1891. His pictures were on
show with Whistler's portrait of his mother.
(You know the people will consider, or used

to consider Whistler as eccentric.) I was then
told that our Frenchman was going to our
Islands and then Tati told me about him.
Very little to me; perhaps more to you. After
that accidentally I came across some letters
of his, later published in some review, written
from Tahiti. They were meant to be expressive of a return of the over-civilized to Nature. They were very foolish and probably
very much affected but also naïve and, I think,
truthful. I never remembered to get the whole
of them — I mean the letters. He described
his meeting some of our ladies, the Queen in-
cluded, and some of his quotations of conversation were parlous. Still you know that
the ladies are essentially feminine and will do
anything they d—— p——. Then there
were descriptions of sunsets and the water and
mountains and what evidently strikes even
such as you and me.

"And he did n't like the French of course,
and he had no money or little, or made believe to have little, and he went into the wilderness and lived the simple life — the cocoa-
nut and bread-fruit life — with some relative
companion to charm the simplicity of food,
etc. All that seemed natural enough; stupid

enough; and yet there was something of the man who has found something.

"Then somebody sent me a catalogue of an exhibition of his.

"I have no doubt that your description of the Frenchman's paintings, which I understand you have not seen, must be quite accurate if one could be accurate about the peculiar shows which some of those good people indulge in. I say indulge in; I mean that they are driven to do something to attract attention. Even their own attention.

"I abandon this tedious subject to say that I had not heard that Mrs. Gardner had bought the Rembrandt. . . . I have no objection any more than you to her buying the Rembrandt for £30,000, but I wish instead that last year she had bought the big, naked woman that Velasquez painted. Or rather, no; I wish the picture had been bought for some place here where we could see it often. I saw it fifty years ago. It was strangely wonderful and almost uninteresting, but as a good lesson for students I should have much recommended it if I remember rightly; and I say this with the fear of Mr. Comstock hanging over me. Certainly it was the picture of a lady without any clothes on and I never knew whether it was prose or poetry. At any rate, it was all the more wonderful, for those good boys, the Spaniards, were so strict and puritanical about painting anything in the slightest way dubious."

There is something very appropriate to our study of La Farge about that transition from Gauguin to Velasquez. Accidental enough, it is still symbolical of his invariable return from the work that passes to the work that endures. And even in the presence of the masters he maintained his clearness of judgment, distinguishing between the one essential thing and all that which might be regarded as surplusage. In the summer of 1906 we were both abroad and he wrote to me from Paris, speaking of illness, but suggesting that we might nevertheless explore some galleries together. The letter contains this luminous revelation of his point of view : —

"If my eyes and the remainder of me get better, it would be a pleasure to be with you and perhaps even to look at works of art. Though I must own that as I get older, I am much less curious about seeing anything new. It is strange in one way, but in another I sup-

pose that it means that one grows reasonable.
Our Japanese friend Okakura wrote to me
once from Seville, where, as he said, he was
listening to the songs of the nightingales and
the cries of the gulls. He said that he had abandoned his party of commissioners sent over by
the Japanese Government; all museums, he
said, were the same; all curators of museums
were the same; he had seen two hundred
Rembrandts and two hundred more would not
teach him any more about the importance of
this very great master. And I feel very much
like our Japanese friend. I should almost prefer to see again one of the great paintings, in
fact, I wish I owned one for, let us say, a week;
after that, one might not begin to look at the
thing. Whitney offered me once a little Raphael to keep for a time, but the idea of a painting as large as my hand on my mantelpiece
which had cost $150,000 made me nervous.
I should have had to put it on my mantelpiece
in that lower apartment of the same house you
are now in. All this has its meaning which you
will understand."

As it happened our paths did not cross, but
when at home again in the fall he told me
of his travels and especially of his last day in

Paris, which he had spent with his doctor. The latter he described with much interest as such a thoroughly French type, a doctor first but full of intelligence about other things. He gave a large part of his day to his patient and they spent some of their time in the Louvre. La Farge got a guide and promised to pay him five francs extra if he would not open his mouth but would take them straight to the particular pictures that he, La Farge, remembered and wanted to see once more. It was all very delightful. It pleased him especially to see the Rubenses again, in a room that was not a gallery but really a room, and he mused over the idea of a banquet given amongst those glorious canvasses with all the guests in historic costume. The last thing that he looked at was in the room of the French Primitives, the amazing "Dead Christ" from Avignon. As they came out of the building the Doctor said, "Wait, I can tell you what your emotions were and how the pictures stirred you. I have felt your pulse. It has gone up according as you have been pleased." He told La Farge which pictures had affected him, and how, and there was no mistake in his report. "The most exciting of all," he said, "was the 'Dead

Christ' — *that* was a shock." "And," said La
Farge, "he was right."

There we have the clairvoyance of which I
have spoken, his marvellous sensibility, the
man who, as I have said, was the artist pure
and simple. And yet here again we must turn
back and recognize his complexity of soul,
noting how emotion was with him saturated
in intellect, how he ranged from the world of
imagination to the world of solid fact, and os-
cillated between ideas of intangible beauty and
ideas of recorded things. In one of his letters
to Mr. Adams he speaks of a decoration upon
which he is at work and says, "I don't know
that you'd like it. It is frightfully realistic —
as if I had known Justinian and Trebonian
quite well, just like other people, which, of
course, is on one side quite absurd." It was his
way, in his work, to come thus to close quarters with the figures of the past. It was the
same in his dealings with literature. Witness
these passages from another letter to Mr.
Adams : —

"I am doing some reading, if I can so call it.
I am trying Plutarch again. I am all the time
astonished at my ignorance and loss of memory with regard to anything. I wonder some-

times how much you keep of your historical
reading. By the bye, have you ever seen
among those lovely letters of Henri IV one
addressed to his wife, Marie de Medici, about
Plutarch? He writes from on board ship. He
has gone out from Havre, I think, being offered a sail by the High Admiral, with some
little meaning to it in the way of armament
and war, and there being little to do he takes
a volume of Plutarch, which he likes to have
by him, and which he recommends to Marie
— whether ironically or not, who could guess
behind his smile of irony and good nature? If
you can lay your hand on the letter, do read
it; I have it not by me.

"Did I ever tell you one of my first impressions of Europe was having in my hands a lot
of Henri IV letters to an old Protestant companion in arms? You, of course, have gone
through all that sort of thing, as it were, by
ancestral obligation, and the handwriting of
the illustrious must have been familiar to you
early."

With this I must give another fragment
illustrative of La Farge as a reader, for it is
also — and in this peculiarly characteristic —
illustrative of him as an artist. It occurs, again,
in a letter to Mr. Adams: —

"I can't pity you for having read all Plato. I've made a shy at it several times these last five or six years and have always come to grief. Summer before last I took up the original at the beginning of the 'Republic.' I owed it to Socrates that painting him, I should do the best I could to be with him, see something of him. Besides you know that he was a sculptor and his talk is very much like studio talk, though better than what I usually get — to-day! Well, I broke down on that first Greek page. Of course I knew all that it meant — having read it many times, but I could not read it properly.

"I was reading it in my son John's copy, annotated by himself. He came in fresh from Europe, and then he too could not read the whole page right through. A few years had made that difference to him as a great many years had made to me. I shall have to try Plato again; I can always enjoy him by skipping, but to read it right along shows me that I never was meant to follow the meanderings of philosophers — I mean the system-makers. I tried Aristophanes last year and got a good deal out of him, not all of poetry and deep or shallow meaning, but also I was tempted to

understand a little of the story of ordinary
Greek life. So that I cannot pity you as your
letter seems to require."

In the foregoing words, and in many others
like them, La Farge has told us in this volume
much of his thought on literature and on art.
Much, too, concerning himself in his work
has been set forth in his own language. One
question, as I draw near to the close of my
narrative, remains to be answered. What was
his feeling about his career, about his work, as
he looked back over it all? I know that it was
a feeling of happiness in fine things achieved,
of modest pride. A great artist knows when
he has effectively put forth his strength. Old
age and illness could not quench in La Farge
his joy in his genius, his consciousness of the
beauty he had brought into the world. But
throughout I have sought, wherever possible,
to give his own reflections on what he had
done, and here, on one of the most interesting
questions in the study of his character, I am
enabled, through the kindness of Mr. Adams,
to cite from a letter to him what is in some
sort La Farge's artistic testament:—

"As you accuse me, I still retain an interest
in pictures, but not so great as when I had

seen fewer. Now one can hardly escape them in our good city of New York, as you will see when you drive up Fifth Avenue.

"My own pictures interest me somewhat, as you remark. Some day I may do them for fun merely. If you remember your history you will remember that the Cat Princess on retiring into private life only killed mice for fun. I kill my mice for living, as she did before her great success. But there is always some pleasure in the hunt. . . .

"Perhaps I could answer that difficult problem you have put to me as to whether it would be better to destroy everything we ever did before we go. . . . One cannot judge for others, exactly, nor do I think for oneself very safely. . . . As far as my experience goes I don't think it is worth while.

"Summer before last fire managed to burn up my work and Saint-Gaudens's at St. Thomas's Church. So that I had an idea of how I should like to have my work destroyed. In this case I felt very badly because it seemed to me the only large piece of work — I mean painting — which I had a chance of doing, and which represented what I thought I could do in the art of painting, which is one of con-

tinuous development; and I had done something new which nobody else had done, and
which I to-day would not feel bold enough to
undertake. Nobody in the future will ever
know what I have done.

"The view depends upon what we wish to
have remain of ours. As Napoleon said, 'It is
rather a poor immortality,' but we cannot
imagine ourselves non-existing. An absolute
cessation is most difficult to grasp; and yet
the Frenchman wrote: —

" Sous la tombe où il dort que fait au grand Ho-
       mère,
Que son nom soit fameux, ou qu'il ne le soit pas ?

"I sometimes think that I shall be, or am,
pleased at leaving some work which has turned
the corner of art in some way and of which I
feel confident as having marked distinctly a
character in the arts. But even the development of the art of glass which I accomplished
seemed to me a small matter while I did it, yet
I feel how small it might be compared to what
I could do if, like Rodin or Chanler, I did not
have to catch mice to eat. You remember that
when Whitney asked me to do glass for him
and 'do my damndest,' I told him that he had

not money enough to pay for what I *could* do :
that I should only do what I thought was fairly
fitting.

"From the point of view which may not
have come up to you, a religiously attuned
mind might desire a manner of destruction of
the ambitions which might appear too earthly.
You may remember that a French sculptor,
Girardon, certainly no slouch, was pleased to
think that he had not been a success. That, I
suppose, was a relic or touch of Port Royal. I
must look him up; I mean his life and traditions. There is no record of Fra Angelico
having destroyed any of his frescoes or other
pieces of work."

These reflections, written in 1906, are
prophetic in their philosophic calm. As his
strength diminished and illness recurred he
faced the inevitable end with an equable spirit.
His soul's affairs were in order and he was confident of the future lying in the dark. He was
content and unafraid. It was a lesson in thinking fortitude to see him, as I did now and then
in the last year of his life, and to hear his still
courageous and, as always, gently humorous
musings on conduct and fate. He spoke of
these things, as for years I had known him to

speak on everything, with wisdom, with char-
ity, and with that keen but somehow detached
interest of his, the interest of the artist, to
whom a problem of morals was as stimulating
and as amusing as a problem in painting or
glass. And in his personal applications of the
spiritual ideas we discussed two golden elements were clearly perceptible, his humility
before the Divine power and his unshakable
dignity. He knew, as I have stated early in this
book, that he had borne no malice toward any
of his fellow men, and, using his unerring sense
of proportion in the contemplation of his own
career, he felt that where he had been faulty
he could meet the last assize with a consciousness that the balance had somehow been re-
dressed. Meanwhile, he kept loyally at his
work, snatching for it every spark of energy
that was left him. But the burden was too
heavy. There came a nervous breakdown and
then great weakness. He was tired out. At
Providence, Rhode Island, on Monday, No-
vember 14th, 1910, he sank to rest. On the
following Thursday, the 17th, the funeral services were held at the church of St. Francis
Xavier in New York and his body was taken
to a vault at Woodlawn.

La Farge's mind was, in his own phrase,
"religiously attuned." The fact is writ large
across his work. It was by a kind of inner spiritual right that he entered the innumerable
churches he decorated. He labored therein
much after the manner of the mediæval craftsman, the craftsman of an age of faith. I say
this, too, with a full realization of the fact that
not all of the edifices he embellished, by any
means, belonged to his own communion. But
like his old grandmother, Madame Binsse de
Saint-Victor, he was indisposed to make much
of the details of worship. For him belief and
cleanliness of soul were the main things. He
could not have been a bigot if he had tried. His
respect for the beliefs of others was illimitable.
I remember his telling me with much picturesque detail of his coming across certain dis-
creetly veiled survivals in the South Seas of
the cult for "long pig," and of the social traditions they still preserved amongst divers
chiefs and their followers. Whatever was monstrous in the subject was so obvious as to be
taken for granted. La Farge could dispassion-
ately appreciate, nevertheless, the point of
view of his islanders. He was far from de-
liquescing, however, into an attitude of ami-

able condonation. His intellect might range,
but his soul was set upon a rock. And, moreover, from his religious inheritance, from the
training of his childhood and youth, he never
wandered. In his generation, more perhaps
than in our own, the church played its part
from day to day in a man's life. It was not
separated in his thoughts from his other interests but was intertwined with them and
affected their development. I have shown him
in his young manhood sympathetically for-
gathering with Paul de Saint-Victor and his
rather pagan friends, but he was equally at
home in very different circles. Recalling his
pre-Raphaelite intimacies he told me that he
immensely liked Christina Rossetti. She was a
personality, he said, maintaining that it was as
she put herself into her poetry that she made
it interesting. They used to talk together about
religion, and, he said, "She must have thought
me a very spiritual person. It was odd, but I
could tell her things she didn't know about
Romanism, which was blurred for her by her
father's Dantean, anarchistic ideas and the
pressure of things English around her." No
pressure around him could wean La Farge
from the church into which he was born. As

his son, Father John, told me, he died in the possession of a lively Christian faith — and it was the faith of his fathers.

It was the faith, too, of that European civilization toward which in so many of the relations of his life he instinctively turned, the faith, through the centuries, of men like himself. "The man of imagination," says Matthew Arnold, "nay, and the philosopher, too, in spite of her propensity to burn him — will always have a weakness for the Catholic Church, because of the rich treasures of human life which have been stored within her pale." It was through this human power, as through her purely spiritual authority, that the Roman Church drew La Farge to her bosom, and he found repose there, too, by virtue of his accord with historic tradition. When Velasquez died King Philip and his courtiers, paying tribute to him as to a great painter, paid tribute to him also as to one of themselves. They buried him as a Knight of the Order of Santiago. So it was fitting for La Farge to carry to his grave, affixed to his coat, the insignia of the Legion of Honor, mute symbol of his kinship with France and thereby with the ancient order of things. He was, in truth, a representative of that order, and his death may be said to have snapped a link between the art of America and the art of Europe in its Golden Age.

He was our sole "Old Master," our sole type of the kind of genius that went out with the Italian Renaissance. To say this is no disparagement of those other creative artists whose names give lustre to our annals. It is simply to suggest his alliance with a specific tradition, the tradition of men such as Leonardo and Raphael. Like them he was a type of intellect governing and coloring imagination and emotion and expressing itself with a certain natural tendency toward the grand style. Overlaid upon this central strength of his were all the riches of a wonderful personality, all the traits of a man whose feeling for the past never for a moment detached him from the current of modern life. His was probably the most complex nature in our artistic history, and, indeed, he had in this respect no parallel among the masters of his time abroad. And every impulse of this myriad-minded man was an impulse toward beauty. That it was which gave value to his work and endued him with an incomparable charm.

His fame is largely that of a great colorist, who made his mark in monumental mural decorations and in windows of stained glass. In both these fields he was wont to illustrate noble subjects, and the loftiness of his ideas was also made known through his easel pictures and through his essays and addresses on painting. He had repute as a traveller, gained through his enchanting souvenirs of Japan and the South Seas. His outstanding character as a painter and as a worker in glass has been enriched and made the more beguiling in the public mind by the sense of his versatility, of the grace and the originality with which he touched many interests. Yet the La Farge to whom I would above all pay tribute is the La Farge who was, in a sense, greater than all of his works, the La Farge who was, to those who knew him well, a lambent flame of inspiration.

There was something Leonardesque about him, something of the universal genius. There was probably no subject of interest to man which was not of interest to him. He drank of civilization as one drinks from a bubbling spring. He knew it in those aspects which belong to antiquity, through all the long story

which stretches down from Greece and Rome
and the immemorial East to our own day of
industrialism and politics. Side by side with
the mundane transactions of humanity his
mind sought to keep pace with the philoso-
phies and religions of the world. It was not
with any pedantry that he assimilated his
knowledge of these things — or used it. It was,
rather, with the ardor of a thinker having an
incurable zest for the soul's experience that
he constantly read and thought, and read and
thought again, until his intellect was a very
cosmos of sensations. Out of it poured his
paintings and his other works, for he was ever
the artist, the maker, the man who must put
his ideas into tangible form; and out of it there
came also what I can only describe as a fertilizing force, a spirit immanent in everything
that he did and vivifying his unforgettable
talk, a spirit making him a singular instance
of constructive power. When we lost him we
lost a great character.

FINIS.

INDEX

About, Edmond, 77.

Adams, Henry, 16, 164, 190, 212, 226, 233, 234, 237, 244, 250, 251, 253.

Alma-Tadema, L., 37.

Angelico, Fra, 108, 256.

Architectural League, the, 224.

Aristophanes, 252.

Arnold, Matthew, 260.

" Ascension," The, 161, 208.

Baltimore decorations, the, 181.

Balzac, H. de, 12, 57, 72.

Bancroft, John, 121.

Barre de Nantueil, Vicomte de la, 46.

Barnes, Grace Edith, 35, 37, 89, 90, 131, 232.

Bartholdi, Auguste, 154.

Barye, A. L., 70, 149.

Baudelaire, C., 77.

Bing, M., 193.

Blake, William, 138, 243.

Blanc, Charles, 69.

Boccaccio, 52.

Bode, Dr. W., 38.

Boissier, Gaston, 25.

Bonaparte, Joseph, 46.

Booth, Edwin, 138.

Bossuet, 56.

Boughton, G. H., 109.

Brattle Street Church, Boston, 154.

Brooks, Phillips, 158.

Brown, Ford Madox, 137, 187.

Bullard, Francis, 188.

Burne-Jones, E., 87, 186.

Burnham, D. H., 230.

Byron, Lord, 31, 57.

Cadwalader, J. L., 230.

Cellini, 218.

Chanler, R., 255.

Chassériau, Th., 84, 104.

Chavannes, Puvis de, 25, 85, 93, 96.

Chevreul, M. E., 87.

Confucius, 181.

Congregational Church, Newport, 220.

Conway, Sir M., 86.

Corday, Charlotte, 80.

Corneille, 57.

Corot, J. B. C., 128, 229.

Courier, Paul Louis, 57.

Couture, T., 89, 91, 93, 96, 110, 117, 243.

David, J. L., 82.

Delacroix, E., 31, 85, 96, 100, 104, 149, 186, 238.

Derby, Dr. R. H., 188, 195.

Dewing, Maria Oakey, 133.

Donald, Dr. E. W., 162, 227.

Diaz, N., 70.

Du Fais, John, 159.

Duff, Sir M. E. Grant, 77.

Dupré, J., 104.

Durand-Ruel, M., 185.

Durer, 69.

Fantin-Latour, H., 133.

Félix, Lia, 76.

Flaubert, G., 77, 134.

France, Anatole, 25, 100, 134.

Fromentin, E., 238.

Gambrill, Richard, 109.
Gardner, Mrs. John L., 115, 246.
Gauguin, P., 244, 247.
Gautier, Th., 77, 83.
Gavarni, 77, 100.
Gebhart, E., 25.
Gérôme, J. L., 84.
Gilbert, Cass, 172.
Girardon, F., 256.
Goncourts, the, 75.
Goya, F., 243.
Grandville, J., 56.
Grenier, E., 78.
Guérin, P. N., 82.
Guerrier, General, 43.
Guilbert, Melanie, 80.

Hecker, Father, 120.
Heine, H., 72, 136.
Henri IV, 41, 251.
Henri V, 57.
Hobbes, John Oliver, 3.
Hokusai, 235.
Homer, 56.
Homer, Winslow, 70, 183.
Houghton, Mr., 138.
Hugo, Victor, 77.
Huneker, James, 242.
Hung Ai, 143.
Hunt, R. M., 109, 153.
Hunt, W. M., 96, 110, 119, 132, 158.
Huysmans, J. K., 33.
"Hynerotomachia Poliphili," 188.

Incarnation, Church of the, New York, 160.
Ingres, J. A. D., 82, 84, 100, 104.
Inness, George, 71.

James, Henry, 35, 117.
James, William, 117.
Johannot, Tony, 57.
Johnson, Dr., 37, 233.
Johnston, Humphreys, 19.
Joncquière, J. de, 41.
Josephine, Empress, 57.
Jowett, Benjamin, 176.

Kaiser, the, 37.
Keats, John, 207.
King, Clarence, 26, 198.

La Farge, Father John, 252, 260.
La Farge, J. F. de, 43, 52, 57, 73, 79, 90, 97.
La Farge, Mrs. Margaret Mason Perry, 120.
La Fontaine, 52.
Lamartine, 74, 78.
Landor, W. S., 40.
"Last Valley, The," 186.
Lathrop, Francis, 159.
Le Bon, G., 221.
Leclerc, General, 43.
Lemoyne, J. B., 63.
Leonardo, 261.
Lever, Charles, 60.
Loti, Pierre, 25.
Low, A. A., 122.
Luther, 53.

Maistre, J. M., de, 80, 81.
Mantegna, 24.
Marat, 80.
Maroncelli, 59.
Martin, Homer, 71.
Matthews, Brander, 239.
May, Edward, 91.
Maynard, G. W., 32, 159.
Mazzini, 60.

McKim, C. F., 188, 225, 230.
McKim, Mead & White, 224.
Medici, Marie de, 251.
Michael Angelo, 36, 210, 225, 235.
Millet, J. F., 84, 96, 111, 116, 229.
Millet, F. D., 159.
Mocquard, J. F., 76.
Molière, 57.
Monet, C., 185.
Moreau, G., 85, 210.
Musset, A. de, 72.

Nadar, 74.
Napoleon I, 53, 57, 60, 255.
Napoleon III, 60, 155.
Newman, Cardinal, 68.
Normanby, Marquis of, 40.
Norton, C. E., 188.

Okakura, 18, 22, 103, 124, 166, 181, 248.

"Paradise Valley," the, 122, 127, 129, 132, 156, 208.
"Peacock Window," the, 199, 208.
Pellico, Silvio, 59.
Piombo, Sebastiano del, 64.
Pisanello, 24.
Plato, 175, 252.
Plutarch, 250.
Post, G. B., 109, 152.

Rachel, 45, 76.
Racine, 57.
Raphael, 75, 107, 248, 261.
Reid Music Room, the, 161.
Reinach, Salomon, 25.
Rembrandt, 94, 108, 124, 235, 246.

Renan, Ary, 183.
Renan, E., 25, 77.
Richardson, H. H., 152.
Rimmer, Dr. W., 142.
Rochambeau, Admiral, 65.
Rodin, Auguste, 38, 149, 255.
Rome, King of, 57.
Rosa, Salvator, 63.
Rose, G. L., 159.
Rossetti, Christina, 259.
Rossetti, D. G., 38, 137, 186.
Rossetti, W. M., 137.
Rousseau, Th., 96, 118, 128, 186, 229.
Rubens, 95, 98.
Ruskin, J., 68, 72, 82, 86.
Ruysdael, S., 64.

Sainte-Beuve, C. A., 77.
Saint-Gaudens, Augustus, 20, 22, 32, 162, 204, 229, 231, 254.
St. Paul decorations, the, 138, 172.
St. Thomas's Church, New York, 160, 204, 229, 254.
Saint-Victor, Binsse de, 44, 50, 56, 62, 64.
Saint-Victor, Madame Binsse de, 50, 58, 258.
Saint-Victor, J. B. de, 50, 79, 86.
Saint-Victor, Paul de, 50, 74, 83, 86, 126, 259.
Sand, George, 134.
Sargent, J. S., 157.
Scudder, Horace, 137.
Smith, S. L., 159.
Socrates, 14, 252.
Stendhal, 80.
Stevens, Alfred, 144.
Stillman, W. J., 109.

Strange, Henry Le, 89.
Sturgis, Russell, 29.
Swinburne, A. C., 231.

Taine, H., 236.
Ticknor and Fields, 137.
Tintoretto, 210.
Titian, 36, 98, 210.
Toussaint, 43.
Trinity Church, Boston, 153, 156, 228.
Troyon, C., 70.
Turner, J. M. W., 57, 72.

Uchard, Mario, 77.

Van Brunt, H., 109, 186.
Vanderbilt house, the, 204.
Van Horne, Sir W., 115.
Vedder, Elihu, 132.

Velasquez, 98, 107, 246, 247, 260.
Vernet, H., 63.
Victoria, Queen, 154.
Viollet-le-Duc, 88, 153.
Voltaire, 56, 57.

Ward, J. Q. A., 232.
Ware, William, 109, 186.
Watson Memorial Window, the, 183.
Watteau, 161.
Watts, G. F., 210.
Wellington, Duke of, 220.
Whistler, 13, 19, 31, 123, 136, 207, 233, 238, 244.
White, Stanford, 117, 163, 224.
Whitney, W. C., 143, 248, 255.
"Wolf Charmer, The," 139, 142.
Wormeley, Miss K. P., 12.

The Riverside Press
CAMBRIDGE . MASSACHUSETTS
U . S . A